Conversations with Joyce Carol Oates

Literary Conversations Series

Peggy Whitman Prenshaw
General Editor

Courtesy *Esquire;* © Norman Seef

Conversations
with Joyce Carol Oates

Edited by
Lee Milazzo

University Press of Mississippi
Jackson and London

Library of Congress Cataloging-in-Publication Data

Oates, Joyce Carol, 1938-
    Conversations with Joyce Carol Oates.

    (Literary conversations series)
    1. Oates, Joyce Carol, 1938-   —Interviews.
2. Novelists, American—20th century—Interviews.
I. Milazzo, Lee.   II. Title.   III. Series.
PS3565.A8Z465   1989   813'.54   89-16673
ISBN 0-87805-411-1 (alk. paper)
ISBN 0-87805-412-X (pbk. : alk. paper)

British Library Cataloguing-in-Publication data is available.

Books by Joyce Carol Oates

By the North Gate. NY: Vanguard Press, 1963.

With Shuddering Fall. NY: Vanguard Press, 1964.

Upon the Sweeping Flood and Other Stories. NY: Vanguard Press, 1966.

A Garden of Earthly Delights. NY: Vanguard Press, 1967.

Expensive People. NY: Vanguard Press, 1968.

Women In Love and Other Poems. NY: Albondocani Press, 1968.

Anonymous Sins and Other Poems. Baton Rouge: Louisiana State University Press, 1969.

them. NY: Vanguard Press, 1969.

Cupid and Psyche. NY: Albondocani Press, 1970.

Love and Its Derangements: Poems. Baton Rouge: Louisiana State University Press, 1970.

The Wheel of Love and Other Stories. NY: Vanguard Press, 1970.

Woman Is the Death of the Soul. Toronto: Coach House Press, 1970.

Wonderland. NY: Vanguard Press, 1971.

The Edge of Impossibility: Tragic Forms in Literature. NY: Vanguard Press, 1972.

In Case of Accidental Death. Cambridge, MA: Pomegranate Press, 1972.

Marriages and Infidelities: Short Stories. NY: Vanguard Press, 1972.

Wooded Forms. NY: Albondocani Press, 1972.

Angel Fire: Poems. Baton Rouge: Louisiana State University Press, 1973.

Do With Me What You Will. NY: Vanguard Press, 1973.

Dreaming America & Other Poems. NY: Aloe Editions, 1973.

The Hostile Sun: The Poetry of D. H. Lawrence. Los Angeles: Black Sparrow Press, 1973.

A Posthumous Sketch. Los Angeles: Black Sparrow, 1973.

Scenes From American Life: Contemporary Short Fiction. NY: Vanguard, 1973.

The Girl. Cambridge, MA: Pomegranate Press, 1974.

The Goddess and Other Women. NY: Vanguard Press, 1974.

The Hungry Ghosts: Seven Allusive Comedies. Los Angeles: Black Sparrow Press, 1974.

Miracle Play. Los Angeles: Black Sparrow Press, 1974.

New Heaven, New Earth: The Visionary Experience in Literature. NY: Vanguard, 1974.

Plagiarized Material. Los Angeles: Black Sparrow Press, 1974.

Where Are You Going, Where Have You Been?: Stories of Young America. Greenwich, CT: Fawcett, 1974.

The Assassins: A Book of Hours. NY: Vanguard Press, 1975.

The Fabulous Beasts: Poems. Baton Rouge: Louisiana State University Press, 1975.

The Poisoned Kiss and Other Stories from the Portuguese. NY: Vanguard Press, 1975.

Marya: A Life. NY: Dutton, 1986.

The Miraculous Birth. Concord, NH: William B. Ewert, 1986.

Raven's Wing. NY: Dutton, 1986.

Blue-Bearded Lover. Concord, NH: William B. Ewert, 1987.

The Time Traveler. Northridge: Lord John Press, 1987.

You Must Remember This. NY: Dutton, 1987

Lives of the Twins (under the pseudonym of Rosamond Smith). NY: Simon & Schuster, 1987.

On Boxing. NY: Doubleday, 1987.

The Assignation. NY: Ecco Press, 1988.

Reading the Fights (with Daniel Halpern). NY: Henry Holt, 1988.

(Woman) Writer: Occasion & Opportunities. NY: Dutton, 1988.

American Appetites. NY: Dutton, 1989.

The Time Traveler: Poems. NY: Dutton, 1989.

Soul/Mates (under the pseudonym of Rosamond Smith). NY: Dutton, 1989.

Contents

Introduction

Writers are most often compared to other writers and their works to various styles in the literary tradition. The work of Joyce Carol Oates, however, can best be compared to the cyclorama, an art form popular in the nineteenth century, for during the past twenty-five years Oates has given readers nothing less than a modern panorama of American life.

One of the most popular forms of visual entertainment and instruction in its time, the cyclorama was an ingenious device that allowed eager viewers to see both the overall contours and specific details of great historical (and sometimes contemporary) events. The founding of the nation, the struggle for independence, the Civil War, the winning of the West—these and more were portrayed on cycloramas that traveled from tiny hamlets to small towns to large cities throughout the United States. The enormous pictures distorted reality for artistic effect, but the studied misrepresentations really did not matter to audiences because the cycloramas showed them individuals and episodes they would otherwise never see.

As for Oates, her vast canvas is filled with tellingly precise details. Her more than sixty books demonstrate a remarkable versatility of style and subject. Oates's first book, *By the North Gate* (1963), focuses on rural western New York state; *Expensive People* (1968) describes suburban America through the eyes of a boy genius who is also a murderer; *With Shuddering Fall* (1964) portrays the intense love affair between a seventeen-year-old girl and an older racing car driver; *them* (1969) depicts the disintegration of a major urban area into lawlessness, looting and rioting. Since these early successes Oates has continued to paint her picture of America past and present, for as she once said, "I certainly do have a general plan for my writing." Thus *Do With Me What You Will* (1973), a gripping story of adulterous love and marriage, is also just one of "a number of novels, one after another, that deal with the complex distribution of power in the United States." *Wonderland* (1971) centers on Oates's notion of the "bizarre connection between the grossly cruel economics of a competitive system and the psychology of 'medicine' "; *Son of the Morning* investigates the power that fanatical evangelical churches hold over individuals and society; and *Do With Me What You Will* examines today's aristocrats, those who practice and interpret the law.

American myths have occupied Oates even in her series of parody novels. Although she has half-humorously called *Bellefleur* (1980) her vampire novel, this huge gothic speculation on the tragedy of greed in the Gilded Age is in her words actually a microcosm of America, "imperialist, exploitative, yet tirelessly optimistic." Similarly, Oates enlarged the scope of her "romance" novel, *A Bloodsmoor Romance* (1982), to comment on those numerous forces—transcendentalism, radicalism, spiritualism, industrialism—so prevalent in the nineteenth century that retain their power over us even today. Yet it is in her most popular novel, *You Must Remember This* (1987), that Oates most forcefully and most faithfully captures the America recognized by so many readers. The sunshine of Ike's smile, assuring us that everything is OK; the ghostly flicker of the newfangled television sets, hypnotizing millions into believing that life really is one big Ozzie and Harriet show; the whirl of hula-hoops, confirming the happy-go-lucky nature of the times—these are the images that define the 1950s for today's readers.

Of course, the so-called Placid Decade was much more than even the sum of these events. Oates's portrayal of the Stevick family of Port Oriskany, New York, reveals the confusion and desperation that marked the attempts of so many to conform to the decade's rigid standards and at the same time to escape them. *You Must Remember This* is thus a sometimes shocking novel that examines the lives of people unable (and often unwilling) to discern the differences between the great American dream and the equally potent American nightmare.

On another level, *You Must Remember This* remains perhaps the clearest artistic expression of a credo Oates described to interviewer Dale Boesky: "I could not take the time to write about a group of people who did not represent, in their various struggles, fantasies, unusual experiences, hopes, etc., our society in miniature."[1] Her focus on this theme in her work is a recurring topic throughout the interviews collected in this volume. Yet, as these interviews taken from a wide variety of sources (*Newsweek, The New York Times, Contemporary Literature, Publisher's Weekly, Harper's Bazaar*) over a considerable period (1969 to 1988) demonstrate, Oates is no mere chronicler of American society. If her works were simply photographically realistic snapshot albums, they long ago would have been relegated to the same dusty shelves that hold the largely forgotten fiction of Sinclair Lewis and John O'Hara.

It is Oates's deep commitment to art, another theme of these interviews, that distinguishes her work. Readers familiar with her novels, short stories, poetry, plays and essays know Oates to be a consummate literary artist.

Some critics have disagreed, of course, citing the seemingly unremitting violence that appears to dominate Oates's work and complaining about her prodigious output. In reply Oates suggests that one of the main yet misunderstood responsibilities of the artist is "to bear witness—in an almost religious sense—to certain things," including "the experience of the concentration camps . . . the experience of suffering, the humiliation of any forms of persecution." It is no surprise, then, that Oates's move to Detroit in the early 1960s changed her life dramatically, for there she saw first hand the racial unrest that culminated in the violent disturbances of 1967. The personal violence in some of Oates's fiction—the murder in *Expensive People*, the horrors of "The Triumph of the Spider Monkey" (1976), the criminal cases in *The Mysteries of Winterthurn* (1984)—frequently has an unreal or surreal quality, almost as if the characters are detached from it. In other instances, however, the violence is strong, vivid and immediate. The abuse endured by Marya in the novel of the same name (1986), the beatings suffered by Wesley Sterne in "The Precipice" (1978), and the psychological bullying accepted by Monica in *Solstice* (1985) are but a few examples of the violence that marks the everyday lives of so many people. Oates once said, "A writer's job, ideally, is to act as the conscience of his race. People frequently misunderstand serious art because it is often violent and unattractive. I wish the world were a better place, but I wouldn't be honest as a writer if I ignored the actual conditions around me."

Interestingly enough, Oates believes that part of the criticism leveled at her use of violence is a "sexist response," for as she explained to Michael Schumacher, "It may well have seemed even to responsible critics that a woman's natural artform was needlework; hence, any deviation from this genteel activity was alarming." Those same skeptics have expressed dismay at Oates's fascination with boxing, but as she explained to George Vecsey, "I'm probably as horrified by boxing as you are. I'm also mystified by it." Perhaps what intrigues her is the monastic side of boxers' lives, their ability to shut themselves off from human contact and expose themselves to public and private pain, as so many artists have done.

Oates is always forthright in discussing her productivity. To Leif Sjoberg, she countered the charge that she writes too much by reminding him that "the older, healthy tradition of the writer as an extremely hard-working and persistent craftsman is no longer fashionable. It appears that I am somewhat unusual, but measured against Balzac, Dickens, Henry James, Edith Wharton, Dostoevski, and many others, among the serious writers, I am certainly not unusual." According to Walter Clemons, Oates once said, "I have a laughably Balzacian ambition to get the whole world into a book."

Most interviewers ask Oates about her writing habits, of course, and readers will find a striking consistency in her answers. Even more surprising, at least to some critics, will be Oates's explanations of how she initially composes in longhand (her detractors claim she must dictate) and how carefully she rewrites everything (some faultfinders hint that she seldom retouches her work). As she says, "I'm very dependent on working in longhand. All my poetry and most of my novels are taken down in longhand first." Oates also told Schumacher that "I revise endlessly, tirelessly—chapters, scenes, paragraphs. . . . The pleasure is the rewriting." She even changed the ending of *Wonderland* for the English edition, published after the American printing, because she was still dissatisfied with the original conclusion.

Perhaps the best clue to understanding Oates's style lies in her statement that she feels a kinship with Virginia Woolf in aiming for what Woolf called a surface of "fluidity, breathlessness, spontaneity." Although Oates's style is clearly her own, she readily acknowledges the influence of Faulkner, Kafka, Freud, Mann, Dostoevski, Melville, Proust, Stendahl, Sartre, Flaubert and Katherine Anne Porter. Oates even told Clemons, "I just see myself as standing in a very strong tradition and my debt to other writers is very obvious. I couldn't exist without them."

In more than one interview Oates notes the primacy of poetry in her writing. "The poems are therefore shorthand, instantaneous accounts of a state of mind that might have been treated in a 400-page work," she explained to the *Ohio Review*. At the same time, Oates believes that poetry is "a rite involving language—at its very highest a sacred rite in that it transcends the personality of the poet and communicates its vision, whether explicitly or by indirection, to others."

This sense of the power of art to communicate, illuminate and instruct is the heart of Oates's conception of literature. To a question about her definition of art, Oates replied, "Art is magnificent, divine, because it records the struggles of exceptional men to order their fantasies, their doubts, even their certainties, into an external structure that celebrates the life force itself, the energy of life, as well as the simple fact that someone created it—and especially the fact that you, the audience, are sharing it." Oates carries her fervor for literature into her teaching and her public readings. The most telling comment about her teaching is that of the student who said she wished the class would never end. Those who have seen Oates read know that Rita D. Jacobs's account of how she "lights up in front of an audience" is an understatement. Oates may put her audience at ease with a few initial humorous remarks, but she soon relies on the power of art to create that same "mystical affirmation or common bond" with her audience that she achieves in her writing.

Yet Oates is a practical artist, though that is a poor phrase indeed to describe her work. Not for her are the verbal pyrotechnics of high modernism, the deliberate obscurities of Joyce, Pound or Eliot. Rather, Oates seems to construct her work so that it will appeal to general readers as well as more literary ones. Part of Oates's appeal, of course, is her style, which she adapts to the subject at hand; part is her keen visual sense, which allows readers to see individuals and events in a new light; and part is her ability to tell a story, which is still the primary ingredient in fiction.

These interviews clearly reveal Oates's dedication to her art. Indeed, they present a vivid picture of the writer as the conscience of society, of the creator of memorable prose and poetry, of the artist deeply committed to a unique vision. But the conversations also provide glimpses of Oates the individual patiently (often humorously) answering such standard questions as "where do you work," "when do you write," "how long does it take you to finish a long novel," "what are your hobbies," "are you married" and "how many more books do you plan to publish." The result is a rich portrait of Joyce Carol Oates, artist and woman.

I wish to thank my assistants Bryan S. Dauphin and Mark A. Johnston, without whose dedicated efforts this project would not have been completed. And special thanks to Joyce Carol Oates for her gracious cooperation in allowing these interviews to be published.

LM
August 1988

1. Dale Boesky, "Correspondence with Joyce Carol Oates," *International Review of Psychoanalysis,* 1975, pp. 481-86.

Chronology

1938   Born in Lockport, New York

1945-52   Attends one-room school in rural community outside Lockport

1956   Graduates from Williamsville (New York) Central High School. Enters Syracuse University.

1959   Co-winner of *Mademoiselle* college fiction award for short story "In the Old World"

1960   Graduates from Syracuse University, Phi Beta Kappa and class valedictorian. Enters graduate English program at University of Wisconsin.

1961   Marries Raymond J. Smith, fellow graduate student at Wisconsin. Receives master's degree from University of Wisconsin. Enters Ph.D. program in English at Rice University.

1962   Discovers one of her stories cited in Honor Roll of Martha Foley's annual *Best American Short Stories* and decides to become writer

1963   Instructor of English at University of Detroit until 1967. Publishes first book *By the North Gate*, collection of short stories.

1965   Premiere of *The Sweet Enemy* at Actors Playhouse, New York

1967   Professor of English at the University of Windsor until
        1978. Receives O. Henry Prize Story Award for 1967 and
        again for 1968. Guggenheim Fellow 1967-1968.

1968   Wins Rosenthal Foundation Award of the National In-
        stitute of Arts and Letters

1970   Receives National Book Award for *them*. Premiere of
        Sunday Dinner at St. Clement's Church, New York.

1972   Premiere of *Ontological Proof of My Existence*, Cubiculo
        Theatre, New York

1973   Premiere of *Miracle Play*, Playhouse II Theatre, New York

1974   Cofounds *The Ontario Review* with husband Raymond
        Smith

1978   Member American Academy and Institute of Arts and
        Letters. Writer-in-residence and professor of English at
        Princeton University.

Conversations with Joyce Carol Oates

Joyce Carol Oates at Home

Walter Clemons/1969

From *The New York Times Book Review*, 28 September 1969,
4-5, 48. © 1969 by *The New York Times Book Review*. Reprinted by permission.

If you haven't yet read Joyce Carol Oates, the chances are that you
have been meaning to, that you have a vague notion she is Southern
(wrong) and that her books seem to have been appearing with
unusual velocity over the past few years (quite right).

Her first, *By the North Gate* (1963), was a collection of stories,
most of them about the hard lives of rural people in "Eden County"
in western New York State. Reviewers casting about for comparisons
came up with Eudora Welty, Willa Cather, Katherine Anne Porter and
William Faulkner, among others.

By general agreement a 25-year-old writer had made a remarkable
debut, and it was followed the next year by *With Shuddering Fall*, a
highly charged first novel about a destructive love affair between a
sheltered 17-year-old girl and a rough racing-car driver. Next came
Upon the Sweeping Flood (1966), a second collection of stories even
better than the first.

Joyce Carol Oates began to reach a wider audience with *A Garden
of Earthly Delights* (1967), a big three-generation novel that traced its
heroine's progress from a childhood in migrant workers' camps to the
security of a middle-class marriage; it ended in explosive violence
and her subsequent decline in a nursing home. At least one critic was
reminded this time of Dreiser. *Expensive People* (1968) moved into
new territory: glossy suburbia as seen by a fat boy-genius who told
how he came to murder one of his parents. Reviewers praised, and
found things wrong with, both these ambitious novels; both were
nominated and were strong contenders for National Book Awards.

Meanwhile Miss Oates went on writing stories that have turned up
regularly in the *O. Henry Prize Stories* (First Prize in 1967 for "In the
Region of Ice") and *Best American Short Stories*; and she found time
because Frank Corsaro urged her to, to write a play, *The Sweet
Enemy*, that was produced off-Broadway in 1965.

them, reviewed on this page, is her fourth novel, sixth book, in six years. She is all of 31.

She turned out to be a frail, shy-voiced girl with soft, dark eyes—she is so gentle that if you met her at a literary party and failed to catch her name, it might be hard to imagine her reading, much less writing, the unflinching fiction of Joyce Carol Oates. She and her husband, Raymond Smith (whom she met and married when they were graduate students at the University of Wisconsin almost nine years ago) both teach in the English department of the University of Windsor, Ont., across the river from Detroit. Their house is on the riverfront drive a few miles from the university, with a back terrace overlooking a lawn that slopes down to the water. Belle Isle is visible directly across the river, with Grosse Pointe in the distance off to the right.

It is very quiet here, and in good weather she may sit for hours on this terrace or on the pier at the foot of the lawn. "I write in a strange way, I don't know if this is interesting to you. . . ." Encouraged to explain, she says, "It's mainly daydreaming. I sit and look out at the river, I daydream about a kind of populated empty space. There's nothing verbal without it. Then there comes a time when—she snaps her fingers soundlessly—it's all set and I just go write it. With a story it's one evening, if I can type that fast."

Her daydreaming before she puts a word on paper has so clarified what she wants to say that she doesn't do much rewriting. "I'm astonished when I hear of writers doing five and ten drafts." Of her writing students she says, "I encourage them to waste time," adding with a smile: "They like that. But then, they may write something. I encourage them to try writing in all kinds of moods, when they're tired and their guard is down. When they're depressed. I hesitate to put it this way, because I'm impatient with 'mysticism,' but I do rely, I guess, on a kind of mystical imagination."

How did she begin writing? "I always have, always wanted to." She grew up in the country, one of three children, outside the small city of Lockport in western New York. The family was Catholic, her father a tool and die designer. She went to a one-room elementary schoolhouse, then to city schools for junior and senior high, and to Syracuse University on scholarships. There she took a writing course under Donald A. Dike, who introduced her to Faulkner's work, the first great influence on her own writing.

"I was bowled over by Faulkner. I haven't reread him in several years, but I will this year—I'm teaching *The Sound and the Fury.* Then Kafka. Kafka I've continued to read." Later: "Freud, Nietzsche, Mann—they're almost real personalities in my life. And Dostoevsky and Melville. Stendhal is a later discovery. And Proust.

"And Sartre's *Nausea.* You've never read it? I know it doesn't sound it, but it's such a happy novel. A religious novel in a way I can understand religion."

Though an early story of hers, "In the Old World," was a co-winner of a 1959 *Mademoiselle* college fiction award while she was still at Syracuse, she hadn't enough confidence then to think of a career as a writer. After her year of graduate work at Wisconsin she accompanied her husband to his first teaching post in Beaumont, Tex.—not her favorite place in the world. (A central character in *them* undergoes a sticky visit to Beaumont.)

She commuted by bus to Rice University in Houston to start work on her Ph.D. in English and in the library there came upon the newest volume of Martha Foley's *Best American Short Stories*, with one of her stories cited in the year's Honor Roll at the back of the book. "I hadn't known about it until I just picked it up and saw it. I thought, maybe I could be a writer. . . . I went back to Beaumont on the bus and stopped thinking about a Ph.D. Later I wrote Martha Foley a letter to thank her. . . ."

She now has what she calls "a laughably Balzacian ambition to get the whole world into a book. John Barth has wanted to do that, I think. John Updike may have had that in mind in *Couples.* I'm Updike's ideal reader, and John Cheever's." Saying this seems to make her shy again: "I don't mean that presumptuously. Only that whatever they write I read immediately, and I read it again two or three times." She is enthusiastic about John Fowles's forthcoming *The French Lieutenant's Woman,* calling it "a real novel, a Victorian novel." She likes the solidity of 19th-century fiction and is comically disappointed that *them,* which she hadn't seen in book form until today, is only 500 pages. "It was 700 pages in manuscript. Well, next time."

We walk down the lawn to the pier. Is it possible to swim here? "You can," she says. "I don't. This river is dangerous, it doesn't look it. I'm not very sporty, not in the water anyway. I play tennis some." It has come up in conversation earlier that she will not travel by air. It is the penalty of a powerful imagination, one guesses in listening to her, that it will not stop working and can populate an empty, ordinary landscape with unwanted violent events. Far out on the sunny river a small blue boat is rocking gently with two boys in it. She says softly, "I don't like to see them out there. Those boats turn over very easily and you can't get them upright again. If that happened, I'm not sure what I could do."

She turns back to the terrace. She has a book of poems coming out next month, called *Anonymous Sins*, and then a book of critical essays, *The Edge of Impossibility: Forms of Tragic Literature*. Later there will be another book of stories. "I experiment more in stories than I do in novels. I don't like to bother Blanche—" (Blanche Gregory, her New York literary agent) "with things that won't make her any money," and so she mails out many of these herself, to small literary magazines around the country. Since her last collection in 1966, 75 or more have been published, she isn't sure how many. "I can only put 10 or 15 of them into a book."

And she has begun a new novel.

An Interview with Joyce Carol Oates

Linda Kuehl/1969

From *Commonweal*, 5 December 1969, 307-310. © 1969 *Commonweal*. Reprinted by permission.

Joyce Carol Oates, at 31, has begotten four novels, *them, Expensive People, A Garden of Earthly Delights, With Shuddering Fall*, and two volumes of short stories, *Upon the Sweeping Flood, By the North Gate* (all Vanguard Press). Numerous other stories have appeared in magazines and anthologies. She has published a volume of poetry (Louisiana State University Press), and next spring Vanguard will bring out *The Edge of Impossibility*, a collection of her critical essays.

This formidable output has won Miss Oates two nominations for the National Book Award, several O. Henry Prize Awards, a Guggenheim Fellowship and National Institute of Arts and Letters grant. While producing poetry and fiction at such great speed, she also teaches creative writing and continental literature at the University of Windsor, Ontario. A devoted sailor, like her husband, a professor of 18th-century English literature, she lives in a beachfront home on the Canadian border across the river from Detroit, the setting of her latest novel, *them*.

them is written in a fairly naturalistic manner, yet charged with nightmarish quality. It depicts a poor white family: tough, resilient mother; sensitive, politically radical son; fragile, tortured daughter. The novel culminates with the 1967 Detroit riots, the author's apparent attempt to show, in wider social terms, the inevitable consequences of the poverty, violence and futility which dominate the lives of people like the Wendalls.

Q: *Your preface identifies your latest novel as "a work of history in fictional form." Was the creative process altered by having facts at hand—facts that you were recording?*

A: Yes, I think definitely, because I felt that I must always be responsible to a certain dimension that could be verified or found

7

fraudulent. I imagined this novel as a series of events that have more or less historical validity. The events did not necessarily happen in the order that they occur in the novel. They did not all happen to the same people, but they happened to people whom I either had known or had heard about or had read about in the newspapers, so that most of the novel is very real.

Q: *Is Maureen Wendall—who is based upon a real person, a former student of yours—is she like your other precious heroines?*

A: I don't think of Maureen as being very energetic. She's rather passive. One thing that happened to her—and it's really the worst thing that happened to her in the whole novel—is when she lost that stupid secretary's book. This is something that had happened to me too, and both of us responded in a very weak, rather victimized way, by being annihilated almost and reduced to tears and despair by a completely foolish event which is so small and yet, when you're that age, it can sort of run over you. I think a strong person—I'm not a strong person, she's not either—a strong, impulsive child would have been affected much, oh, much more mildly by that event.

Q: *In most of your other work, there seems to be a dichotomy between your neurasthenic, sexually backward male characters and your tough, daring females.*

A: I think the dichotomy is more between intellectual and non-intellectual people rather than between male and female. At the end of *A Garden of Earthly Delights*, Swan is in love, in a way, with a cousin of his who has been in and out of the novel earlier and she is like him. She is rather weak and too . . . too self-conscious, I suppose, is the word. I have a great admiration for those females who I know from my own life, my background, my family—very strong female figures who do not have much imagination in an intellectual sense, but they're very capable of dealing with life. I think that in my writing I really admire these people and keep coming back to this kind of personality which is completely antithetical to my own.

Q: *How do the male figures like Swan and, of course, Richard in* Expensive People *fit into this particular scheme?*

A: They tend to be more intellectual and, I think, they're rather autobiographical. I project my doubts, my metaphysical and philosophical doubts, into them. That's why they erupt into violence more often.

Q: *Yes, Richard shoots his mother and Swan his stepfather. Is this the natural outgrowth of a Freudian triangle? Or did you ever think of it as such?*

A: Domestic romance? Yes, *A Garden of Earthly Delights* does have that, though it's not really a triangle. It's more between the boy and his mother. Strictly speaking, to have this Freudian romance, one must have a good strong father figure, so it's not quite that, but . . . but close to it, I think.

Q: *Why the patricide or matricide in the novels?*

A: These novels are put together in parallel construction. Each deals with a male imagination and consciousness that seeks to liberate itself from certain confinements, and only in the last novel, *them*, does this consciousness really become liberated in what I see to be an ironic way, that an act, a gratuitous act of murder, is committed, and this frees the individual. He's on his way to some sort of American success whereas in the other two novels it didn't work. In *them*, I saw Jules as a kind of American success in an ironic sense, of course. He is a hero and a murderer at once. I think that is ironic. I hope it is. Maybe it is a common thing. Really it's very difficult to answer these questions because, although you're bound to make perfect sense or perfect nonsense within the context of the novels, it's hard to talk about them in an analytical manner.

Q: *You can't do that to your own fiction?*

A: I don't think that one could really do that to fiction at all. That if we were to discuss Hamlet or Alyosha Karamazov and discuss these people outside the context of their world, they would make sense, because we are comparing them to more ordinary behavior in the normal context.

Q: *You've been called a gothic novelist. Do you agree?*

A: I don't know what those words mean. I use words myself in a kind of loose manner. One has to use language to communicate, though the words often don't mean anything. I'm really a romantic writer in the tradition of Stendhal and Flaubert.

Q: *In the tradition of any American novelists?*

A: I'm like Melville, I suppose. There's a similar, certain clumsiness and bluntness and a blindness toward excess which I think I share with him.

Q: *Not Faulkner?*

A: I think I'm like Faulkner. I suppose he's gothic . . . naturalistic . . .

Q: *And Flannery O'Connor?*

A: I don't know. I used to think that I was influenced by O'Connor.
I don't know that I am really. She's so religious, and her works have
to be seen as religious works with this other rather creepy dimension
in the background, whereas in my writing there is only the natural
world.

Q: *There's no Catholic or religious influence?*

A: I think of religion as a kind of psychological manifestation of
deep powers, deep imaginative, mysterious powers which are always
with us. And what has been in the past called supernatural, I would
prefer simply to call natural. However, though these things are
natural, they are still inaccessible and cannot be understood, cannot
be controlled.

Q: *But you don't see any direct Catholic influence as you do in
Flannery O'Connor?*

A: I think there probably is a great deal there that I'm not owning
up to. I know my first novel, *With Shuddering Fall*, was conceived as
a religious work. Where the father was the father of the Old Testa-
ment who gives a command, as God gave a command to Abraham,
and everything was parallel—very strictly parallel—and how we can
obey or not obey it, and, if we do obey it, we're not going to get
rewarded for it anyway. I think I was working myself out of the
religious phase of my life and tried to show that having faith in this
larger context leaves one really nowhere. One has defeated the world
and defeated one's own impulses and passions and is left with
nothing—sort of like a nun. I hadn't thought about that novel for
many years. It's very disturbing to me, some of the things that went
into it. It was very personal and very, in many ways, very autobiographical.

Q: *Everything you treat seems in some way to be tinged with
irony.*

A: I don't do that consciously. I try to write things with happy
endings, but they seem to turn out bathed in a kind of green light that
I didn't imagine.

Q: *Does irony have anything to do with disavowing Catholicism,
that it grows out of your rebellion in a religious sense?*

A: That might be, though I don't think of myself as rebelling. I think of Ivan Karamazov who returns the ticket and his brother says, "That's rebellion." And Ivan smiles sadly and says, "Well, I hadn't thought of it that way." Or, "One can't live in a state of rebellion." But this is a word that somebody else gives to it.

Q: *It's not rebellion?*

A: I don't think so. In any case, one goes on to the next problem which is the problem of living in the world. It seems to me a sufficiently intricate hopeless problem itself without bringing in another world, bringing in an extra dimension. Those of us who are intellectuals, so to speak, and who deal with intellectual and literary matters, have forgotten if we ever knew the toughness of the world where there isn't any money. This is the basic reality. It's economic.

Q: *Your first two novels and most of your short stories take place in Eden County. Is that fictitious?*

A: Yes. It's really nowhere, nowhere at all.

Q: *Is Eden County your paradise lost?*

A: I'm from a county that's called Erie County which is in western New York, near Buffalo and Lockport, not too far from the Great Lakes. So I imagined the county named Eden with just certain similar elements. I don't know that it's paradise lost.

Q: *In other words, your choice of Eden was not because of the* Garden of Eden?

A: I suppose I had that in mind. I think so. I was very interested in religious problems when I was writing those early stories, and many of them I know I had imagined as workings out of remarks of Pascal, and also Kafka, and Kierkegaard too. And I would take ideas from these men and try to illustrate them dramatically.

Q: *There is the motif of free will.*

A: I don't really know what free will means, but it's something we all think about every day of our lives. We never come to any conclusions. We think we're free. We think we're liberated or about to be liberated. It comes home to us that we're not at all free. It's a continual mystery. I really don't think we come to the end of it. It's exciting not to come to the end of something.

Q: *It's amazing that you can write a novel a year.*

A: I really write more than that. It's just that only one is published a year. Usually I'd written another novel in between that I don't

publish, so that novels as they come out don't represent strict chron-
ological order. I write the ones I don't publish with great enthusiasm. I
love them when I'm writing them, and then they're all done. And so I
write another novel which I love, but I like the second one better than
the first, so the first one I don't submit to publication. I just keep it at
home, because you tend to like the things that you've written most
recently.

Q: *They come in pairs?*

A: No, they just all go along, one after the other. I have one at
home that I wrote . . . I can't remember exactly when. That's about
400 pages and it has lots of references to the Vietnam War. And I can
see that if I don't publish that soon it's going to be completely out of
date, or I'll just have to change it to the war in Thailand or something.
But it's so heartbreaking. When I wrote that novel, I said these events
really took place in 1969, and I had written it in 1968, and dated it
ahead thinking, well, this will be just right. But now it's going to be
1970. This novel I probably will never publish. It's a long love story. It
takes place in Detroit and Grosse Point, but the Vietnam War is very
real to the people who are in the novel.

Q: *How about your latest? Is this novel one you intend to publish
or put away?*

A: I don't have a latest novel. I'm working on a collection of short
stories about a central theme. I've been doing that lately. I have a
whole lot of short stories about love—different forms of love, mainly
in family relationships: mothers, fathers, sisters, brothers, and that sort
of thing. So that's what I've been working on and I think that will
come out in the fall of 1970. It will be called just *Love Stories*. And I'll
be starting another novel which I hope will be published in 1971 if I
finish it.

Q: *Do your books need a lot of editing?*

A: No. I don't change much around. I shorten some things. That's
about it.

Q: *Is poetry as demanding as novel writing?*

A: It's much more immediately rewarding, and there's nothing as
wonderful as writing a poem, even a bad poem. It's just wonderful to
have this small unit, a work of art, complete on a page before you.
With a short story, particularly with a novel, it's much more of a linear

thing, and it takes longer just to get through it. So the psychological reward is just a little more diffused. It's not as dramatic.

Q: *Your dust jackets say you live "a life that is a study of conventionality."*

A: Yes, I am very conventional. My husband, Raymond, and I are very ordinary, happy people and I thought I should apologize for it. I didn't have any long list of things like busboy, Western Union boy, short-order cook, naval officer—all of those things that are on most people's dust jackets. So I sort of apologized.

Q: *Then to take Maureen or Clara or Karen—all very unhappy characters—as the author is most unrealistic?*

A: No, they're not me at all. I think if I were in their position I would behave the way they do. I may be some day in the position that those people are in. Robert Lowell, in the Introduction to *Notebook*, said that writing about the journal of a very complex year in his own life and the life of the United States—how did that go?— that somehow the sorrow got in the poems but not the happiness. It's so weird and baffling. You just have to be an extraordinary artist to put in happy endings.

Q: *Would you like to?*

A: I don't know that people need happy books because a happy book is like a happy person—there's nothing to be said about it, nothing to be done to it or for it.

Hunger for Dreams

Paul D. Zimmerman/1970

From *Newsweek*, 23 March 1970, 109-110. © 1970 Newsweek, Inc. Reprinted by permission.

For a time it seemed that Joyce Carol Oates was destined to be a bridesmaid but never a bride. In 1968, her *A Garden of Earthly Delights*, the saga of a migrant family's rise to middle-class respectability, was one of the nominations for a National Book Award. The prize went to Thornton Wilder's *The Eighth Day*. The following year, Miss Oates's *Expensive People*, a Gothic tale set in suburbia, was nominated for the NBA prize, but *Steps* by Jerzy Kosinski was chosen by the judges. This year Miss Oates finally captured the NBA garland with *them*, a brilliantly resourceful novel of a working-class white family growing up in Detroit.

Passion is Miss Oates's subject—passion and its irrational power over human destinies. *them*, like her other novels, is filled with murder and mayhem—throats slit, heads blown off, crimes of passion and unreason, riots, beatings, prostitution. "Things like that happen every day in Detroit," she says in a voice that is almost a whisper. Her music of violence pours from a slender reed. Miss Oates is quiet, almost timorous, spectrally thin, occasionally remote in self-defense when asked questions that invade her carefully guarded inner life. She endures interviews, her eyes staring away like some trapped bird unable to focus on the enemy. Her diffident, controlled exterior conceals a fiery intensity. Only the pen unleashes it.

She was born 31 years ago in Lockport, N.Y., a small city near Buffalo, where her father worked as a tool-and-die designer. She dismisses her childhood as "dull, ordinary, nothing people would be interested in," not because it was really dull and ordinary but because it was too terrible to talk about. "A great deal frightened me," she says cryptically but will not elaborate.

She was a writer from the very beginning. "I drew stories before I could write. Then I'd pretend to write them, you know, just make-believe writing without real letters." "I was always a good girl," she adds with slight irony. "It's only recently that I've considered other modes of behavior—because of certain cataclysmic events." Some of them have been personal and some social, like the Detroit riots which she describes in *them* with an energy and truth not caught in the endless television and newspaper accounts. Miss Oates herself makes no clear distinction between the personal events that shape her view of things and the public ones. "It's hard to say when one's own personal life stops blending in with the sound of a police siren," she says as a police car passes on the street below. "Cataclysmic events in society are also personal events."

From the beginning, her taste as a writer gravitated toward the Gothic. Her first novel, intended for the juvenile market and written when she was 15, tells of a dope addict rehabilitated by owning a black stallion. It was rejected, but she kept writing—at Syracuse University, at the University of Wisconsin where she met her husband, Raymond Smith. (They both now teach at the University of Windsor in Ontario, across the river from Detroit.) Kafka was among her early influences. "In college, I *was* Franz Kafka for a while."

And her works still float past the reader in dreamlike Kafkaesque images. She writes from her daydreams, letting them percolate into stories. Then she writes them down, "in a state of high psychic energy," on scrap paper. The next day "these disembodied hands that write my stories" type out what she calls "one psychic unit" of prose.

Why does she write? "Oh, I can't tell you that," she says. "You'll write it in the magazine and my husband and friends will read it." She does not, however, feel vulnerable and exposed in the 500 pages of *them*, which she calls "largely autobiographical." "People think they're reading fiction," she explains. "That's why I don't feel exposed. I've fixed it up so my fiction gives me a certain protection."

But, in a sense, she does reveal the source of her prose nightmares when she says: "We all dream. Scientists tell us if we don't dream, we go mad—and then, of course, we become dreamers again. In our dreams, we are all novelists and filmmakers and poets. Some of us have more energy and carry these dreams over from the nighttime. I have a habit of drawing faces and figures and doodling all the time. I don't see any difference between the night dream, the day dream, the doodle, the story and *War and Peace*. They all come from the same impulse."

Miss Oates, who occasionally contributes perceptive and thoughtful reviews to *The Detroit News*, is at work on the first of three novels housed in her mind. "It deals with the madness of crowds," she says. What does she hope her fiction will do for her readers? "I don't know," she answers firmly, her narrow hand flicking away the question. "Art does the same things dreams do. We have a hunger for dreams and art fulfills that hunger. So much of real life is a disappointment. That's why we have art."

The Dark Lady of American Letters

Joe David Bellamy/1972

From *Atlantic*, Fall 1972, 63-67. © 1972 *The Atlantic Monthly* and Joe David Bellamy. Reprinted by permission.

"I feel a certain impatience with generalizations, especially my own," Joyce Carol Oates wrote in her reply to my preliminary questions, mailed off to her just a few days before, "but I'll try to think out coherent answers to your questions.

"Art is mostly unconscious and instinctive; theories obviously come later in history, in personal history, and are therefore suspicious. Any kind of verbal analysis of any kind of impulsive art is dissatisfying. This isn't a way out of answering difficult questions—though I am always eager to find a way out of questions of any kind—but something I believe in very strongly."

Unlike her previous letter, written out in her careful, elegant hand—in which she gave her consent to this interview-by-mail—this letter was crowded onto the page, typewritten single-spaced in shotgun style with "X"ed-out corrections, almost without margins, as if the pages themselves had seemed scarcely large enough to the writer to contain the potential deluge of language—or so I imagined.

This was not the first time I was to be surprised by the promptness of her replies. I was undecided whether to be gratified by this swiftness or simply flabbergasted. Surely she had more pressing things to do than to write to me. Surely she was attending to those pressing matters, whatever they were, in addition to writing these letters. Such productivity struck me as mildly terrifying.

Though hardly out of character. Winner of the 1970 National Book Award for fiction, as well as numerous other prizes for her writing through the years, Joyce Carol Oates has been producing work (especially fiction, but also poetry, plays, criticism, and reviews) at an astounding rate since the publication of her first collection of stories, *By the North Gate*, eight years ago: five novels published, three more collections of stories, two books of poetry, two

17

plays produced off-Broadway, a book on tragedy, on and
on.

The interview which follows is an edited version of our
correspondence, including all material that seemed perti-
nent to a consideration of the writer and her work. Aside
from a few minor alterations made for the sake of greater
coherence or accommodation of the material into an interview format, the questions and answers are reproduced as
originally written.

Joe David Bellamy: What are your writing habits? What times of
day do you like to write? How many pages do you average—if there
is an average? How do you manage to write so much? Is this simply
natural facility, or have you cultivated it in some unusual way?

Joyce Carol Oates: I don't have any formal writing habits. Most
of the time I do nothing, and the fact of time passing so relentlessly is
a source of anguish to me. There are not enough hours in the day.
Yet I waste most of my time, in daydreaming, in drawing faces on
pieces of paper (I have a compulsion to draw faces; I've drawn
several million faces in my life, and I'm doomed to carry this peculiar
habit with me to the grave). We live on the Detroit River, and I spend
a lot of time looking at the river. Everything is flowing away, flowing
by. When I'm with people I often fall into a kind of waking sleep, a
daydreaming about the people, the strangers, who are to be the
"characters" in a story or a novel I will be writing. I can't do much
about this habit. At times my head seems crowded; there is a kind of
pressure inside it, almost a frightening physical sense of confusion,
fullness, dizziness. Strange people appear in my thoughts, and define
themselves slowly to me: first their faces, then their personalities and
quirks and personal histories, then their relationships with other
people, who very slowly appear; and a kind of "plot" then becomes
clear to me, as I figure out how all these people came together and
what they are doing. I can see them at times very closely, and indeed
I "am" them—my personality merges with theirs. At other times I can
see them from a distance; the general shape of their lives, which will
be transformed into a novel, becomes clear to me; so I try to put this
all together, working very slowly, never hurrying the process. I can't
hurry it any more than I can prevent it. When the story is more or

less coherent and has emerged from the underground, then I can
begin to write quite quickly. In *Wonderland* (published in October,
1971) I did about the same number of pages on certain days; in fact
last summer, working in a kind of trance, elated and exhausted, for
many hours at a time. I wasn't creating a story but simply recording
it, remembering it. This is true for all of my writing; I have never
"made up" a story while sitting at the typewriter. But then, of course,
there is revision.

Bellamy: What are you working on now?

Oates: I am putting together a group of short stories called
Marriages and Infidelities, which include stories that are re-imaginings
of famous stories (for instance, "The Dead," "The Lady With the Pet
Dog," "The Metamorphosis," "Where I Lived and What I Lived For,"
"The Turn of the Screw"); and my thoughts are much with this book,
when I am able to get them free of *Wonderland*. ("The Dead" —
retitled by the editors of *McCall's*—was published in the July issue of
that magazine. "The Turn of the Screw" will be out soon in *Iowa
Review*.) These stories are meant to be autonomous stories, yet they
are also testaments of my love and extreme devotion to these other
writers; I imagine a kind of spiritual "marriage" between myself and
them, or let's say our "daimons" in the Yeatsian sense—exactly in the
Yeatsian sense, which is so exasperating and irrational!

Now I am in a state of spiritual exhaustion, I think, from the last
novel I did, *Wonderland*, a novel about brains—the human brain—
which was my most ambitious novel and almost did me in. I had to
read a great deal about the human brain, particularly the pathology
of the brain; I don't recommend it for anyone. Just going through the
galleys brought back to me in a flash all the excitement and dread
and exhaustion of those long days last summer when I wrote the
novel. I couldn't do it again. It might be my last novel, at least my last
large, ambitious novel, where I try to re-create a man's soul, absorb
myself into his consciousness and co-exist with him. In my ordinary
daily life I am a very conventional person, I think—I hope; but while
writing *Wonderland* I found it difficult to keep up the barriers, to keep
myself going as Joyce Smith, a professor of English, a wife, a woman,
with certain friends, certain duties. It is sometimes such a *duty* to
remain sane and accountable. Any study of the human brain leads
one again and again to the most despairing, unanswerable questions

. . . there is no way out of the physical fact of the brain, no way *out* of this confinement. Yet it can't be measured or adequately explained, at least not the relationship between the brain and the "mind" it somehow generates. It has been months since I've finished *Wonderland*, but I can't seem to get free of it. I keep reliving parts of it, not in the way I still relive *them* (I was very fond of Jules Wendall, the hero of *them*), but in another way. It's like a bad dream that never came to a completion. It's the first novel I have written that doesn't end in violence, that doesn't liberate the hero through violence, and therefore there is still a sickish, despairing, confusing atmosphere about it. . . .

Bellamy: *Wonderland* sounds most intriguing. I was interested in what you said about the ending, how there seems to be a connection between its coming back to haunt you and the fact that it *doesn't* end in violence, doesn't "liberate the hero through violence." Do you have any idea why this is so? Or, for that matter, why violence in general characterizes so much of your work?

Related to this, more specific situations occur to me too—for example, a situation in your work where a man is following a woman or where a woman fears or imagines or even possibly hopes a man is following her (but is at the same time repelled); or a situation where a character might be thinking impulsively of suicide. Why do such situations tend to recur? They are inherently dramatic, obviously. Maybe this is a question you don't care to think about, to become conscious about, I'm asking you to do the critic's job really—or even the psychoanalyst's job—on your own work. That's probably not fair. But I do tend to be curious about it.

Oates: I can't do justice to your question about violence; I can't add much to my fiction on this subject. I don't know. Am I personally haunted by the fear of violence, the need for violence, or do I reflect everyone else's feelings about it? I sense it around me, both the fear and the desire, and perhaps I simply have appropriated it from other people. My own life is quiet, very ordinary and conservative; on a scale of 1 to 10 my own energies (id or otherwise) must be around 2, hovering feebly. I sometimes think of how strange it must be to be a man, burdened with biologically determined energies that no one in his right mind would choose. . . . This is the era of Women's Liberation, but I really must say that I think men have a far more difficult time, simply living, existing, trying to measure up to the absurd standards of "masculinity" in our culture and in nature itself, which is so cruel.

Bellamy: Coincidentally, I did read your story after "The Dead" in the July *McCall's*. I did catch the Joyce echo, at the end especially, with the snow falling. It is a strong, intriguing, impressive story. (Since Ilena is a writer and so many of the peripheral details of her life seem similar to your own, I did feel somewhat troubled [actually "embalmed" comes to mind] to learn about her weariness in answering questions about her "writing habits.")

Also, the whole atmosphere of autobiographical confusion, that is, of the mixture of fiction with details that suggested some autobiographical accuracy, was constantly frustrating and amazing and oddly gratifying to my imagination. I suppose it's inevitable that readers develop a sense of curiosity about the personal lives of writers they admire (what else is biography for?). (The question I want to ask here is not, I think, ultimately embarrassing.) Some writers, once they become famous enough (Norman Mailer comes to mind), learn to make good dramatic use of characters similar to or possibly identical to, or even quite different from (but apparently similar to—the reader never knows), themselves. Do you think you were doing something of that sort in this story? (I hope that's a fair question.)

Oates: Some of the details in the story are authentic, some slightly invented, but the general tone of busyness is real enough; except I haven't the aloneness of the character in the story, her freedom to simply be alone once in a while, even if only to think dark thoughts and recall with amazement simpler times.

My use of myself in stories—well, it has always been there, the use of emotions I've felt. I should be a rational, contained person, I guess, but really I am very emotional—I believe that the storm of emotion constitutes our human tragedy, if anything does. It's our constant battle with nature (Nature), trying to subdue chaos outside and inside ourselves, occasionally winning small victories, then being swept along by some cataclysmic event of our own making. I feel an enormous sympathy with people who've gone under, who haven't won even the small victories. . . .

Bellamy: Questions about writing habits *are* probably futile. The implication behind the questions is usually: "Tell me your secret. If I

know how to do it, maybe I will be able to do it." All of this preliminary is unnecessary. I want to ask you a few more simple-minded,
possibly boring questions about your writing habits, and then I won't
bring up the subject again. (a) Do you drink coffee before or while
working? If so, how much? (b) Do you sleep well? How many hours
a night on the average? Do you remember your dreams well—your
nighttime dreams, I mean? (c) Have you ever tried amphetamines or
other sorts of stimulants to help you work better? (I'm thinking of
Ilena in the *McCall's* story and also of John Barth, who said he
sometimes uses a very mild form of speed to help him work better.)

Oates: [This is] a very normal question, which you needn't apologize for, [about] the use of drinks, drugs, coffee, and so on. I don't
take drugs of any kind, or even drink, or smoke (I'm so dull—see
Alfred Kazin's essay on me in the August *Harper's*), or even drink
coffee; it's just the way I happened to grow up, nothing essentially
puritanical and certainly not moral about it. I am addicted to work,
which is to say the expulsion of built-up ideas and formless forms, the
need to get rid of little stories that crowd my head. Alfred Kazin was
quite right in saying that I sometimes write as if to relieve my mind of
things that haunt it, not to create literature that will live. (But I don't
think many writers really work consciously to create literature that will
"live"—that will be monumental, like *Ulysses*. I think most writers
write out of an interior compulsion, hoping that it will add up to an
artistic statement of some worth.) . . . About my dreams: I seem to be
always dreaming, awake or asleep, though when I'm awake I *know*
I'm awake. I wonder if this is normal . . .? My husband evidently
doesn't experience this. Asleep, I dream about anything, just like
anyone else; but I have terrible nights of insomnia, when my mind is
galloping along and I feel a strange eerie nervousness, absolutely
inexplicable. What a nuisance! Or, maybe it isn't a nuisance? An ideal
insomnia allows for a lot of reading. When the house is dark and
quiet and the entire world turned off for the night, it's a marvelous
feeling to be there, alone, with a book, or a blank piece of paper,
even a blank mind, just sitting there alone. Such moments of solitude
redeem all the rushing hours, the daylight confusion of people and
duties. I like to write, but I really love to read: that must be the
greatest pleasure of civilization.

Bellamy: What *do* you read?

Oates: I read constantly, in three areas—the rereading of old works (I'm now going through *Ulysses* again), the reading of an avalanche of literary quarterlies, magazines, reviews, and so on, that come into our home steadily (some magazines are not read but devoured: *New American Review, Tri-Quarterly*, for instance, incredibly good magazines), and new novels. There is a vigor and an excitement in contemporary writing that I think is remarkable. I have only to reach out for any current magazine—let's say *New American Review*, which is handy, issue #10—to discover at least one story that is striking, maybe even a masterpiece. In this issue of *NAR* it is Philip Roth's "On the Air," Kafka and Lenny Bruce and pure Rothian genius, very hard, bitter, terrifying stuff.

Bellamy: What about the future of fiction in general? Do you think the novel may be dead or dying?

Oates: The novel can't be dead or even close to dying if an American publisher can bring out one good novel a year, just one: let's say Bellow's *Mr. Sammler's Planet* last year and Doctorow's *The Book of Daniel* this year. We would hope for more, and we usually do get more.

Bellamy: What sort of possibilities do you see for those fiction writers who are trying to break out of the conventions of the so-called realistic tradition? Are you one of these writers?

Oates: Fiction writers have broken out of the "conventions of the so-called realistic tradition" years ago, decades ago; it's a commonplace of critical thought to point all the way back to *Tristram Shandy* as a convention-breaking work, but even (even!) *Tom Jones* is rather iconoclastic. There has never been a novel so fantastic as *Remembrance of Things Past*. It is all things, a complete life, an extended thought, an arrangement and rearrangement of reality that is much more believable than the reality of most lives lived daily, at least in my part of the world. July 10, 1971, was Proust's one hundredth birthday, and he is very much alive. Another iconoclastic novel is *Dr. Faustus*. What an accomplishment! I am always rereading Mann in utter admiration, in love. Ah, to be able to write like Thomas Mann . . . or even to write a novel that Mann might approve of, even mildly. . . . When I write a story or a novel I don't feel that I am any particular person, with a particular ego. I seem to share, however vaguely, in the "tradition"—the tradition of literature, of all that has been done that I know about and love. Each story has a form and a style that is best suited for it, and all I do is wait around until these things come together—the people in my imagination who are to be the "characters" in the formal work, the form, the style, the language, the setting (which is another character), the mood, the year. So I don't think of myself as "one of those writers who is trying to break free of conventions." There aren't any conventions really. And if *Middlemarch* is a conventional novel, how wonderful it would be if contemporary novelists could write anything comparable! There are no conventions or traditions, only personalities.

Bellamy: Your statement "There are no conventions or traditions, only personalities" I find very liberating and helpful. But I still worry about that question. Of course, fiction writers broke away from the conventions of the so-called realistic tradition years ago; and, of course, the history of the novel can be seen as a series of rebellions against previously "established" forms all the way back to the very beginning. But aren't those rebellions still going on? And if it isn't one writer rebelling against a "tradition," maybe it's a personality rebelling against another personality; or simply any writer working to find something new to keep from boring herself or himself to death.

Maybe what I should have asked was, What sort of presently occurring formal innovations interest you the most? Or, wouldn't you agree that the electric media, for example, have had various sorts of unprecedented influences on contemporary writing? I mean something beyond bothersome prophecies of its demise—formal influences, time-and-space influences? And haven't these affected you? In your own work there seems to be a greater interest in formal experimentation. "The Turn of the Screw" might be one example. In *The Wheel of Love*, stories such as "How I Contemplated the World" and "Matter and Energy," or even "The Wheel of Love" or "Unmailed, Unwritten Letters" (which is much more than a simple epistolary story), seem more formally innovative to me than any of the earlier stories, say, in *By the North Gate*. Why is this?

Oates: I am interested in formal experimentation, yes, but generally this grows out of a certain plot. The form and the style seem naturally suited to the story that has to be told; as in "Matter and Energy" (a story I feel very close to), where the young girl's present life is entirely conditioned by what happened in the past, and her love for a man entirely conditioned—ruined—by her love for her mother, a rotten, hopeless love. Think of the horror, of existing always with the memory of such a mother, committed to an insane asylum—while "you" are free, evidently, to walk around and to act normal, to try to love, to act out a certain role. One always thinks of a few other people day after day; there's no escape. A father, a mother, a few beloved people—that is the extent of the universe, emotionally. And if something has gone wrong inside this small universe, then nothing can ever be made right. (This story is based on the anguished recollections of a student of mine, whose mother is in an asylum and who tried to kill him, many years ago. He is now an adult, an earnest and intelligent young man, but at the same time he is still that child; he is *still* coming home to that mother, to that event.) So the form of that story grew naturally out of its subject matter. In "The Turn of the Screw," the use of journals is a kind of Victorian cliché; among other things, I wanted to suggest how interior lives touch upon one another in odd, jagged, oblique ways, without communicating any essential truth, in fact without communicating truth. In "Unmailed, Unwritten Letters" (which is perhaps my favorite story, at least emotionally), the epistolary form is a way the heroine has of sending out cries for help, not meant to be heard; simply a way of articulating private bewilderment. Not that I want to dwell upon this story, but it seems to have touched some common chord in people—I've received a number of letters from other writers/critics/men of letters of a type, who seem to like it. What does this mean about our American marriages. . . ?

Bellamy: What is your concept of characterization? Or what are your ideas about characterization? This is overly general perhaps (and maybe less coherent than one might hope for). How about this: Do you think "hardened" character such as the kind in Victorian novels is real or valid?

Oates: Your questions about characterization are quite coherent questions, yet I can't answer them because—as you might gather from what I have already said—I don't write the way other people evidently write, or at least I can't make sense of what they say about their writing. My "characters" really dictate themselves to me. I am not free of them, really, and I can't force them into situations they haven't themselves willed. They have the autonomy of characters in a dream. In fact, when I glance through what I have tried to say to you, it occurs to me that I am really transcribing dreams, giving them a certain civilized, extended shape, clearing a few things up, adding daytime details, subtracting fantastic details, and so on, in order to make the story or the novel a work of art. Private dreams have no interest for other people; the dream must be made public, by using one's wit.

People say that I write a great deal, and they are usually curious about when I "find time." But the odd thing is that I waste most of my time. I don't think I am especially productive, but perhaps other writers are less productive. In the past, however, writers like Henry James, Edith Wharton, Dickens (of course), and so on and so forth, wrote a great deal, wrote innumerable volumes, because they were professional writers and writers write. Today, it seems something of an oddity that a writer actually writes, and some writers or critics who don't spend much time writing seem to resent more productive writers. Someone said that John Updike publishes books as often as John O'Hara did, but thankfully his books weren't quite as long as O'Hara's. . . . This is an attitude I can't understand. Any book by Updike is a happy event. The more, the better. If any critic imagines that he is tired of Updike, then he should not read the next Updike novel and he certainly should not review it.

. . . I don't know that the above will strike you as good enough, or that I have answered your questions. I know one thing, though: I would never have thought of some of these things in a person-to-person interview. The whole *social* aspect of such interviewing gets in the way of ideas.

You are kind in the many things you say about my writing and about me (you probably do know me quite well, because I've told you things that acquaintances and social friends of mine would never be told, not in dozens of years)—it may be that I am mysterious, in a way; certainly there are things about myself that don't make sense to me and are therefore mysterious, to me; but the main thing about me is that I am enormously interested in other people, other lives, and that with the least provocation (a few hints of your personal life, let's say, your appearance, your house and setting), I could "go into" your personality and try to imagine it, try to find a way of dramatizing it. I am fascinated by people I meet, or don't meet, people I only corres- pond with, or read about; and I hope my interest in them isn't vampiristic, because I don't want to take life from them, but only to honor the life in them, to give some permanent form to their personalities. It seems to me that there are so many people who are inarticulate, but who suffer and doubt and love, nobly, who need to be immortalized or at least explained.

Here in Windsor, life is filling up with people: parents coming to visit, trunks to be packed, last-minute arrangements to be made, a dozen, a hundred chores, such as what to serve for dinner tonight. But thank God for trivial events! They keep us from spinning completely off into the dark, into the abstract universe.

I hope these answers make some kind of sense to you. Much of this I haven't thought out, until now; it sounds bizarre but is very honest.

An Interview with Joyce Carol Oates

John Alfred Avant/1972

From *Library Journal* [New York], 15 November 1972, 3711-12. © *Library Journal.* Reprinted by permission.

Joyce Carol Oates suggests fragility with reserves of strength behind it. She's slim, birdlike; the voice is soft; the eyes are as riveting, as luminous, as the photographs lead one to expect; the movements are rather prim. Could this actually be the creator of the voluptuous Clara in *A Garden of Earthly Delights*? Was this the novelist who set down the violent horrors of *them* and *Wonderland*? It was indeed, and with her husband Ray Smith. Just off the boat from a year's sabbatical in England, they were spending a few days in New York before returning to teaching at the University of Windsor, Ontario; and they found the garden of the Tavern-on-the-Green pleasantly reminiscent of English settings.

Since Oates reviews books everywhere, we spoke of book reviewing and the reason she is so drawn to the form. "Why, I love to read," she smiles, and remarks that now, rather than review anything she dislikes, she will send back the galleys. Her love for reading carries over into a love for writers; she is saddened when she must dislike other writers' works. Eudora Welty, Robert Coover, Gail Godwin, Stanley Kunitz, Howard Nemerov, John Gardner, John Cheever, J. F. Powers—she has good things to say about all of them. Updike and *Rabbit Redux*? "I didn't like it," she admits, but quickly adds that she liked *Rabbit, Run, The Centaur, Bech: a Book*. Muriel Spark? "Her work has taken a bad turn. One was afraid that Flannery O'Connor, like Spark and other writers strongly influenced by religion, might tighten up in this way; but Flannery O'Connor remained human in her fiction, didn't lose that dimension that Spark has lost."

Oates adores Margaret Drabble, whom she and Ray got to know rather well in England. "Maggie and I seemed to have always known each other. There was an instant response that was highly gratifying." Learning that I hadn't read the latest Drabble, *The Needle's Eye*,

28

Oates promised happily: "You have a treat in store. It's very dense, like a wonderful 19th-Century novel, or like *The French Lieutenant's Woman*."

She has reviewed the new Doris Lessing story collection for *Book World* and talks eagerly about Lessing: "She is a saint; she has gone through everything and has purified herself." We spoke of Lessing's involvement with the Sufi and mentioned related philosophical writers, Gurdjieff and Ouspensky. Oates's response to the awakening interest in Eastern religions is intensely favorable; she has long regretted that the Eastern religious aspect of Thoreau and Emerson is neglected. Later, by mail, she elaborated on the hope that Eastern religion might offer: "One concentrates on something important, instead of trivial goals; America is unfortunately mistaken in its 'goals' of success, but younger people have instinctively rejected these goals (so have their parents, but they feel themselves sadly committed to them and are reluctant to change). The world will be transformed to a newer, more spiritual condition when the wisdom of the East is synthesized with the pragmatic, scientific, efficient technology of the West."

As to Oates's own work, one is eager to know just what she thinks of it, which writers are her conscious influences. "I have a big novel in my head now," she says and makes a gesture like hefting a large package, "that will have many different episodes encompassing the history of America. I'd like to begin it in 1690. In the back of my mind there's a mental picture of *The Brothers Karamazov*, although this novel won't end up resembling *Karamazov* at all. While I was writing *A Garden of Earthly Delights* I had Thomas Mann in my head." Which aspects of Mann? "Thomas Mann, especially in *The Magic Mountain*, dealt with civilization. I wanted to deal with civilization," she says very naturally, giving me rather a jolt, since most readers probably think of *Garden* as primarily a haunting love story, not a parable of civilization. Did she think of the French decadent poets at all in connection with *Garden*? "No," she says, slightly startled, "I've not thought of poetry in connection with my fiction; but, of course, I write poetry too. Ray teaches poetry, you see, and I write poetry." Ray is sitting very quietly, only occasionally adding any comment; but he's very much a part of the afternoon. A low-keyed, attractive man who appears to absorb everything, he nods when

something strikes him as interesting or especially apt; and one can
sense the rapport he and Joyce have. "Ray and I sit up and talk
about poetry a lot, for hours and hours," she says. "So much talk
can sometimes lead you further than you might want to go. Nietzsche
said, 'When you look into the abyss long enough, the abyss looks
back at you.' When you begin to realize this for yourself, it can be
terrifying."

Poetry is obviously one of the centers of Joyce Carol Oates's life.
Although she's not really known as a poet, she refers several times
during the afternoon to her own poetry (two published volumes and
a third coming out soon). Clearly she cares as deeply about the state
of poetry as about the state of fiction. Her forthcoming book of
essays on "modern tragic consciousness" will include one on Sylvia
Plath. "She was a fine poet, with a complete mastery of the
mechanics of poetry. Her view of the universe wasn't accurate, but it
was a complete expression of certain aspects of our consciousness."
For the same collection, she recently wrote "a fifty-seven page essay
on James Dickey, fifty-seven pages." She can't quite believe the
length herself. How long did it take her to write it? "Well, it was fifty-
seven pages; it must have taken several days, but I've thought about
Dickey for a long time."

She's thinking a lot about this book of essays; and she's relieved to
have her next novel, *Do with Me What You Will*, already finished.
"It's a love story, a big novel; and it was easy to write. *Wonderland*
almost did me in." As Oates has also said of *them, Do with Me What
You Will* has its prototypes in real life. She recently became interested
in a Detroit court case in which a judge sentenced a young White
Panther to 15 years for possessing a marijuana cigarette—a charge
that many people thought was trumped up. Joyce and Ray followed
the case, which led to much discussion between them about law. "My
novel is about the law; it's an affirmative book, not such a dark vision
as *Wonderland*." "The law," she says, "is our hope." Later she elaborated: "A transformation of society is possible not through a
rejection of Law, and civilization, but through a humanization of Law;
we must absorb all the risks and outrages of technology into us, and
then move upward to the next level. The anti-rational anti-civilization
movement of the past decade or so in America is sure to be short-
lived, because it is based on an inadequate understanding of how
civilization is really nature—natural—and will evolve according to the

slow, inevitable principles of nature. . . . In the end our natural instincts will guide us to a realization of Being—not through a rejection of the name-and-form confusion of society, but through an absorption of it. Even if people of our generation don't live to experience it, we can be fairly certain that it will occur; hence in a way we can already experience it, imaginatively. And there is surely truth in the observation (Whitman's . . .?) that like-minded people already constitute a paradise of souls."

Oates's fiction may be highly emotional in tone, but it is clearly grounded in layers of thought. Since Oates's pacing is almost always swift and the novels and stories seem quickly written, and since she has said in interviews that she does write quickly and rarely revises extensively, I wondered about the speed at which her highly complex, formally innovative works, such as the new story "The Turn of the Screw," are composed. Did she spend more than her usual amount of time on "The Turn of the Screw," with its two columns of Victorian journals, its Jamesian metaphors, and its elements of Jamesian biography? "No, it was more like typing than writing. But, you see, I had thought it out in my head," she answers simply. "I love Henry James, I love Henry James so much. I wanted to get inside the man."

I mentioned the recent story "The Dead," which is next year's O. Henry-first-prize winner. Its protagonist, both like and unlike what we know of Oates, is a successful young woman novelist who has been nominated for, but not won, a National Book Award; who is a professor of English; who is hooked on drugs and goes desperately from man to man. Oates had just reread the story, and the reading seemed to have been jarring; "my alter-ego," she calls the writer in "The Dead," pushing the air in a backward motion, a kind of silent get-thee-behind-me.

Asked, finally, whether she writes primarily for herself, to purge herself of fantasies, of "alter-egos," or for a certain kind of imagined audience, she replied: "I write for people who are sensitive and somehow related to a web of consciousness that extends outward from them, to other people. I don't write for 'my self'!—unless 'myself' is, like Whitman, some kind of symbolic representation of everyone else. Art should be for the entire species, ultimately, aimed toward an elevation of other people through an extension of their latent sympathies."

Joyce Carol Oates: Love and Violence

Walter Clemons/1972

From *Newsweek*, 11 December 1972, 72-77. © 1972 Newsweek, Inc. Reprinted by permission.

She is a tall, pale young woman with enormous eyes and a timid,
little-girl voice who rather plaintively assures interviewers, "I'm not
that interesting." If you met her at a literary party and failed to catch
her name, it might be hard to imagine her reading, much less writing,
the unflinching fiction that has made Joyce Carol Oates perhaps the
most significant novelist to have emerged in the United States in the
last decade.

At 34, her sweeping vision of America as a delusive wonderland of
colliding forces, where love as often as hate leads to violence, has
established Miss Oates as a major—and controversial—figure in
American writing. Her frailness is deceptive. In less than ten years she
has published five powerfully disquieting novels—*With Shuddering
Fall, A Garden of Earthly Delights, Expensive People, them,* for
which she won the National Book Award in 1970, and *Wonderland.*
There were also four collections of stories, two books of poems, a
collection of essays on tragedy and a couple of hundred book reviews
and stories not yet collected in book form. Three plays have been
produced off-Broadway, and she has finished a fourth. During this
same period she produced two other novels she kept around her
house for a while and finally put out with the garbage. "I thought I
might die and someone might find them," she says cheerfully. "I
don't miss them."

Each of Joyce Carol Oates's books has been a different technical
and intellectual experiment, gradually building up a fictional world
that is recognizably her own. It is a world of such violence that Oates
has often been called "Gothic": 16-year-old Loretta Wendall, early in
them, wakes up to find her lover dead beside her, shot by her
brother, and she is shortly thereafter raped by the policeman who
agrees to remove the body to the alley; the brilliant opening section
of *Wonderland* ends with a boy's escape from a murderous father
who has wiped out the other members of his family.

But Oates is non-Gothic, and original, in her tenacious adherence
to the humble ordinariness that surrounds violence. Her people blot
things out that they can't deal with. "They do not understand . . .
that they have been 'destroyed'," she says. They go on, as dully and
inarticulately as before, and as a result some have found her accounts
of them all too full of verisimilitude. "Events do not build toward a
climax, or accumulate tension and meaning," critic Elizabeth Dalton
complained of *them*. They "simply seem to happen in the random
and insignificant way of real life." But this is the problem that Oates
shares with *every* American writer today—how to bring order to the
violent extremity and complexity of American life without mitigating
that extremity. As Philip Roth has put it: "The American writer in the
middle of the twentieth century has his hands full in trying to understand, and then describe, and then make *credible*, much of the
American reality. It stupefies, it sickens . . . and finally it is even a
kind of embarrassment to one's own meager imagination."

What Joyce Carol Oates has done is to take the novel back to its
root meaning—"news"—in a period when some of the best of her
contemporaries have frankly explored fiction as artifice or turned
from fiction to the New Journalism or to the "nonfiction novel" of
Mailer or Capote. She is nineteenth century in her patient faith that
the novel can show us *The Way We Live Now*, as Trollope called one
of his best books. "I have a laughing Balzacian ambition to get the
whole world into a book," she said when she saw *them* for the first
time in page proofs and was disappointed that it was only 500 pages.
"It was 700 pages in manuscript," mused Oates. "Well, next time."

It is this urgent desire to tell the whole truth about the way we live
that makes Joyce Carol Oates seem so shockproof about today's
shocking world. "It seems that I write about things that are violent
and extreme," she says, "but it is always against a background of
something deep and imperishable. I feel I can wade in blood, I can
endure the 10,000 evil visions because there is this absolutely
imperishable reality behind it."

"Her sweetly brutal sense of what American experience is really
like," as Alfred Kazin has called it, has its source in a period she
cannot remember, though she returns to it regularly in her fiction.
The Depression was almost over when she was born in 1938 in the
town of Lockport in upstate New York, but she feels its effect on her
parents' lives.

"I'm from a part of the world and an economic background where people don't even graduate from high school. My father probably went to about the seventh grade—he had to get out and work when he was 11 or 12, and his whole life has been colored by that, the Depression. And my mother, the same way. But if I have any artistic talent, I think I inherited it from them. My father's always been able to play the violin and the piano—*instinctively.* Where did that come from? And my mother has a domestic artistic talent: what she does with flowers, what she does with the house, her life is an artistic life. If either of them could have gone to college, who knows? But at that point in our economic history, that was out of the question. They were out working, not yet even teenagers. It was a grim, a very grim world."

The world of her childhood—on her maternal grandparents' farm— was grim domestically as well, though she resolutely refuses to go into detail: "Very, very terrible things, that were not sudden but lasted for years, involving long and lingering deaths, cancer . . . and other problems, too. But my mother was a radiant personality, she always was, and I think she's gotten even more so." She put her parents into *Wonderland*; the hero, whose life is shaped by his narrow escape from a murderous father, drives out toward Buffalo and stops near an old cider mill, where he sees a couple and their little girl. "That's my parents and me," Joyce Carol Oates says. "I'm about 4 or 5 years old. There's a snapshot of us in this old swing we had. I thought I'd put us right in the novel, because that's the way I remember my childhood. My father looks out into the lane at this stranger and moves as if to guard and protect his family."

She has always insisted that, except for small details like this, her fiction isn't autobiographical. "I don't really care to write about my own life, because I've already experienced it." But she is emphatic about the importance of her rural childhood. "The thing about me— if—" and she pauses, to put in her customary, embarrassed dis-claimer: "I don't feel I'm that important or interesting." Then she adds: "The real clue to me is that I'm like certain people who are not really understood—Jung and Heidegger are good examples—people of peasant stock, from the country, who then come into a world of literature or philosophy. Part of us is very intellectual, wanting to read all the books in the library—or even wanting to *write* all the books in the library. Then there's the other side of us, which is sheer silence, inarticulate—the silence of nature, of the sky, of pure being."

She was 17 when she entered Syracuse University on a scholarship in 1956, the first member of her family to go to college. Nevertheless, Joyce experienced little cultural shock. "There were many 'farm girls,' as they called us, at Syracuse and I made friends with girls very much like myself, and then on the vacations I brought books back home—my parents were introduced to a world of books, and excitement, through me, simply because they'd sent me there."

Yet one of her most moving early stories, "Archways," describes the plight of students in a remedial-reading course in a state university, "educated now into knowing their unworth." These were "desperate, doomed young people, many of them from the country, remote incidental rural sections of the state," bewildered by the university "so available to them (they, with their high-school diplomas) and yet, as it turned out, so forbidden to them, its great machinery even now working, perhaps, to process cards, grades, symbols that would send them back to their families and the lives they supposed they had escaped."

The defeat that oppresses Joyce Carol Oates's imagination in this story, however, bears no resemblance to her own career at Syracuse. "She was the most brilliant student we've ever had here," says Donald A. Dike, professor of English and Creative Writing at Syracuse, to whom *With Shuddering Fall* is dedicated. He remembers that she wrote mostly short stories, "but about once a term she'd drop a 400-page novel on my desk and I'd read that, too. She had some conscience problems about her writing in those days; she was afraid it was 'not nice' and might offend her parents, and I tried to reassure her."

There is a good-girl, honor-student earnestness about Joyce Carol Oates to this day that baffles and irritates some observers. But there is no doubting her sincerity when she says, "I absolutely don't believe there is very much originality. I just see myself as standing in a very strong tradition and my debt to other writers is very obvious. I couldn't exist without them. I don't have much autonomous existence, nor does anyone. We are interconnected—it seems we are individual and separate, whereas in fact we're not." Her lack of ego amounts almost to an absentmindedness about her own existence.

"My own life just seems to be what I'm doing at the present. If I'm working on a book, that seems to be *the* book, and I can't remember how I did other things."

Her daily life, in fact, bears little resemblance to the turbulent world of her imagination. She and her husband, Raymond Smith, met as graduate students at the University of Wisconsin in 1961 ("at a faculty tea," she remembers, "and we were married three weeks later—it was very romantic"). Both now teach in the English department of the University of Windsor, right across the river from Detroit. Detroit—"so transparent, you can hear it ticking," where she taught from 1962 to 1967, the year of the riots recorded in *them*—is visible from the Smiths' riverside back lawn, but they seldom visit it.

She loves teaching and is good at it. "I wish it would never end," says one student of her course in contemporary literature. Though Joyce Carol Oates has never written a novel about university life, it is the subject of some of her best stories.

One of these is "The Dead," an electrifying study of a red-haired, pill-popping teacher-novelist whose marriage disintegrates as she becomes a literary celebrity. Ilena Williams, lecturing to audiences who "could not see the colorless glop she vomited up in motel bathrooms," says things Joyce Carol Oates has said; Ilena reads from her latest work, "a series of short stories in honor of certain dead writers with whom she felt a kinship." And "The Dead" itself is, of course, a homage to, and re-invention of, James Joyce's famous story of the same title. Ilena is an alternate self, Joyce Carol Oates says, "a way I could have gone. Sometimes a crossroad appears and one can go one direction or the other. Sometimes just writing a story about it, mapping out these directions, saves one from doing it, and maybe in reading it someone else may be saved from it, too."

At home, her electric typewriter is in the bedroom; her husband works in a study just off the living room. One oddity of their quiet life together puzzles an outsider: Ray Smith doesn't read his wife's fiction. "He read *Wonderland*," Joyce Carol Oates says, "and he seemed to like it. He sometimes says, 'Should I read this, honey?' and I usually would rather he didn't. I think I would place such a great, exaggerated value on his word that even a slight twist of an eyebrow—I know him so well—would hurt me and I might feel resentment. I give him things to read, book reviews mostly, impersonal things, and he'll tell me that he likes them. But then I feel, does he really? 'Do you *really* like it?' 'Yes.' 'But do you *really*?' 'Well, yes, but this one sentence, maybe, could be fixed.' And I usually fix it. But I think in a close situation like a marriage it's asking for trouble."

"It's a matter of respecting her privacy," says Smith. "I wouldn't want to inhibit her in her choice of subject matter or in any way. I don't want to stand over her shoulder." It works for them. *A Garden of Earthly Delights, them* and the volume of poems titled *Love and Its Derangement* are dedicated "to my husband, Raymond."

Oates's work habits are as unique as everything else about her. She writes incessantly, wherever she is—while waiting for her luggage on trips, between takes of a NEWSWEEK cover-photo session. Though she writes so rapidly that she sometimes finishes a story in a single evening, she thinks of herself as a slow worker, meaning that she proceeds by periods of "daydreaming" that may last for months before she's ready to sit down at the typewriter. "The novel I'm just about to write now," she says, "I've been working on for a very long time. I've lived through it in my imagination. I know the ending, I know the last paragraph, I know what's going through this person's mind. But I have to find the words to get into it. I woke up this morning with another first paragraph in my head—I've written about five of them. When I get that right . . ." She smiles and snaps her fingers.

Joyce Carol Oates's productivity has aroused irrelevant wonder and impertinent criticism. Her real claim to attention is quite different: the power of her imagination to project her into lives quite different from her own and the fidelity with which she responds to its pressures. The rough world of stock-car racers in *With Shuddering Fall* was convincingly created by a young woman who had never seen such a race and dislikes even riding in cars. "You start from what you do know about speed," she said, "and go on from there. I read a couple of issues of car magazines. And I remembered fairgrounds. I liked walking around them in the winter, when there was nobody around."

The opening scene of *A Garden of Earthly Delights*, in which a group of migrant workers stand in the rain beside a wrecked truck while a woman gives birth, stays in the reader's mind years afterward and doesn't diminish with rereading. In the preface to *them*, her best book, Oates tried to explain how the family recollections of one of her students at the University of Detroit led to the writing of the novel: "For me, as a witness, so much material had the effect of temporarily blocking out my own reality, my personal life and substituting for it the various nightmare adventures of the Wendalls. Their lives pressed upon mine eerily, so that I began to dream about them instead of about myself, dreaming and redreaming their lives. Because their world was so remote from me it entered me with tremendous power, and in a sense the novel wrote itself."

Unlike the macho male tradition of Hemingway and Mailer—the writer as hunter or athlete of experience—Oates belongs to the tradition of insight and imagination. "I guess I experience things in ways I don't understand," she says. "I think I have a vulnerability to a vibrating field of other people's experiences. I lived through the '60s in the United States, I was aware of hatreds and powerful feelings all around me."

She admires Mailer's personal approach. "Mailer has tried to get right out there into the thick of things: he's sought the centers of action, he's put himself physically in the presence of dangers that maybe he glories in. Yet he also wants an intellectual and imaginative distance and I think he's achieved it. I feel these things going on even though I'm not out there physically, and I feel I have to transcribe them—the 10,000 horrible visions you go through to reach the 10,000 beautiful visions. So in a strange way I would compare the attempt—just the attempt—of what I'm doing with Mailer's, though he and I are totally different, totally antithetical, I'm sure, in personality."

Intensely feminine, Joyce Carol Oates is not a doctrinaire feminist; she is a writer first of all, whose sex is neither an issue nor a weapon. Her utter lack of malice and her generosity to fellow authors contrast with the snobbish attitude that many sleek Eastern writers adopt toward her—an attitude summed up by one big female literary name with the dismissive comment: "She's not our sort." One outspoken admirer, however, is Joan Didion (*Play It As It Lays*), a National Book Award judge for 1971 who staunchly supported *Wonderland* for the fiction prize. "I thought it was an extraordinary book," Didion says. "It fascinated me as a writer. The question we all founder on, whether personality has any meaning—instead of theorizing, she just plunged in and dramatized it. She tried for so much more than the other books we were considering."

The first half of *Wonderland*, from the December day on which Jesse Vogel survives the slaughter of his whole family to his escape from a foster-father as grotesque as his real father, is probably the most impressive fiction Joyce Carol Oates has written, inexorable and nightmarishly precise. But the book gave her more trouble, she says, than any of her others. "It was very painful to write. I was able to dramatize the situation in *Wonderland*, but I couldn't resolve the moral questions it raised and that failure distresses me."

As she talks, one realizes that the "moral failure" that is worrying her is the one that has tormented writers before her, most notably Tolstoy: what use is art if it doesn't help people live better? "With *Wonderland* I came to the end of a phase of my life, though I didn't know it," Joyce Carol Oates reflects. "I want to move toward a more articulate moral position, not just dramatizing nightmarish problems but trying to show possible ways of transcending them."

Her recent book of stories, *Marriages and Infidelities*, was intended as a first step in that direction. She once told an interviewer that love was the subject of all her work, and she now says: "I believe we achieve our salvation, or our ruin, by the marriages we contract. I conceived of a book of marriages. Some are conventional marriages of men and women, others are marriages in another sense—with a phase of art, with something that transcends the limitations of the ego. But because people are mortal, most of the marriages they go into are mistakes of some kind, misreadings of themselves. I thought by putting together a sequence of marriages, one might see how this one succeeds and that one fails. And how *this* one leads to some meaning beyond the self."

For all her wading in blood, her unblinking perception of despair in so many lives today, Oates is an optimist. "Blake, Whitman, Lawrence and others have had a vision of a transformation of the human spirit. I agree with it strongly myself. I think it's coming. I don't think it's as close as Charles Reich thinks in *The Greening of America*. He seems to think its imminent—or even that it's already arrived at Yale. I don't think I'll live to see it. But I want to do what little I can to bring it nearer."

In the decade since Philip Roth observed that the violence, vulgarity and unreality of American life baffled any effort to write credible realistic fiction about it, Roth himself has abandoned the effort and resorted to his own highly individual variants: comic monologue, political burlesque and sexual phantasmagoria. And in that same period Norman Mailer has—at least temporarily—committed himself more to nonfiction than to the novel. Impatiently, often, brilliantly, writers of the '60s—John Barth, Donald Barthelme, Thomas Pynchon, Robert Coover, Thomas McGuane and John Gardner—have resorted to parodistic reinventions of the novel, to Borgesian miniaturization, to freeze-dried black comedy as replacements for the realistic narrative that no longer seems feasible to them.

On this fictional scene, Joyce Carol Oates is singular. Though she is as aware as anyone of the possibilities of experimentation and as haunted and oppressed as any of her contemporaries by feelings that American life may be "too much," too crazed, too accelerated to be captured in a novel, she hasn't lost confidence in the power of narrative fiction to give coherence to jumbled experience and to bring about a change of heart. "Let us consider," she recently wrote, "the conclusion of Saul Bellow's *Mister Sammler's Planet*, which is so powerful that it forces us to immediately reread the entire novel, because we have been *altered in the process of reading it* and are now, at its conclusion, ready to begin reading it."

In a letter to *The New York Times Book Review* last summer, she replied with some asperity to a critic who had suggested that she "slow down": "Since critics are constantly telling me to 'slow down,' I must say gently, very gently, that everything I have done so far is only preliminary to my most serious work . . . Every harsh review of my books begins with the routine assessment of my 'output,' in the usual consumer terms. It would be kinder to begin with a recitation of all I have not done . . . owing to our usual human weakness of not expecting enough of ourselves."

She is 34. She has energy, dedication and a stubborn integrity. Like the most important modern writers—Joyce, Proust, Mann—she has an absolute identification with her material: the spirit of a society at a crucial point in its history. She may not produce an American *Ulysses, Remembrance of Things Past* or *The Magic Mountain*; perhaps no writer ever again will, or can, make so huge an act of imaginative appropriation. But in her eagerness to give everything, to absorb everything, "to get the whole world into a book," Joyce Carol Oakes belongs to that small group of writers who keep alive the central ambitions and energies of literature.

Focus on Joyce Carol Oates

Michael and Ariane Batterberry/1973

From *Harper's Bazaar*, September 1973, 159, 174, 176. © 1973
The Hearst Corporation. Reprinted by permission.

Love may be a law unto itself, but Joyce Carol Oates deals
with both Love and Law in her latest novel, *Do With Me
What You Will*, which is coming out next month. Miss
Oates, 35 years old and winner this year of the National
Book Award, is considered by many to be the finest
American novelist now writing. We recently asked her if
she would tell us about her new work . . . and here's what
she had to say.

J.C.O.: "*Do With Me What You Will* is really a love story—a story
about marriage—about adulterous love that leads into marriage. I
hope the novel won't irritate Women's Liberation women who are
somewhat anti-male, because it is, in fact, a celebration of love, and
of marriage . . . since I believe that for most women this path leads to
a higher freedom through the awakening of love, is *the* pathway.
However, there are women who must be independent—who *must*
stand alone. I honor them, and I will write about them another time.
This particular novel is about a woman who falls in love . . . and it is
meant to be an intensely detailed record of the experience of love,
not only from the woman's viewpoint but from her lover's as well."

    A.&M.B.: "Just what led you to write a novel with a legal back-
ground?"

    J.C.O.: "I am writing a number of novels, one after another, that
deal with the complex distribution of power in the United States. In
Wonderland I dealt with a kind of bizarre connection between the
grossly cruel economics of a competitive system and the psychology
of 'medicine,' how the contradictions of our culture (the competitive
ideal vs. the 'love' ideal) lead to a tragic fate, if not examined; in *them*
I dealt with the phenomenon of lower-class attempts to rise, in the
system, possible only through a most ironic twisting of the system's

ideals (struggle, egoistic gain) into criminal activities of one kind or another—outright theft, murder, the stealing of another woman's husband, etcetera. And so to the law: we must acknowledge that the U.S., though set up as a democracy, is in fact an oligarchy. Who are the aristocrats, the elite? What is their profession, their training, where are their degrees from? Who rules on matters of the highest constitutional significance, on a Court that allows one or two men, by swinging a decision one way or another, to have a fantastically widespread effect upon literally millions of people? . . . Lawyers, all. And they have been trained to fight in a system that declares as its first premise an adversary model (that is: prosecution vs. defense, with the ideal of 'justice' totally subservient to the ideal of who can argue best, most powerfully), rather than a model of courtroom procedure that might indicate that 'justice' could be administered through cooperation of some kind."

A.&M.B.: "How much legal research were you obliged to do for your novel?"

J.C.O.: "I did a fair amount of reading for the novel, though no 'research,' and of my personal connections with lawyers, judges, people involved in lawsuits, I cannot speak, for a number of reasons."

A.&M.B.: "What about the characters and events in your new novel? Were they drawn from life?"

J.C.O.: "The novel is fiction, about fictional people, and the Detroit presented—the private clubs, the yacht clubs, the society, the events, the lawyers, the judges—are entirely fictional."

A.&M.B.: "Traditional marriage basically represents a coming together of Love and Law. What do you feel about its partial collapse? About today's divorce laws in general?"

J.C.O.: "Any opinions I have about the legalistic side of marriage are probably insignificant—every state has different laws, and the laws are being changed all the time; one cannot speak of 'divorce law' in America, since it's so complicated. Law is one thing—Love is another, and it can have complications in real life, but in essence it is not complicated at all; it is utterly simple."

A.&M.B.: "Given the power, what laws would you change?"

J.C.O.: "It would be nice to see the laws we have enforced across the board (that is, everyone who possesses drugs be sent to a Maximum Security Prison for 40 years): or, perhaps, a more realistic interpretation of the laws in the Court . . . with an eye toward mercy, not legalistic strategies of simple revenge."

A.&M.B.: "What do you consider the greatest triumphs or miscarriages of legal justice in America?"

J.C.O.: "First of all, Americans must realize that we have a wonderful system of Law in this country, and that our civil rights, our various rights under the constitution, are so valuable, the entire setup so infinitely marvelous in terms of the history of civilizations, and even in quite specific historical terms (compared with English law, for instance, and our own 18th and 19th and early 20th century law), that the country itself is a triumph. But people are always measuring what exists against an ideal, a Platonic ideal of perfection. From one point of view, yes, it was a typical miscarriage of justice that sent Sacco and Vanzetti to their deaths, but from another point of view a wonder that more men like them were not tried, convicted and put to death; and, if we consider other nations, would there have been even a trial . . . ? A public hearing? No. The Watergate affair demonstrates the American capacity for self-criticism and atonement and openness, probably unparalleled in history. But if you get snarled in a certain case, if you're Lenny Bruce (*The People of N.Y. vs. Lenny Bruce* in the mid-Sixties) you're probably doomed: it will do you no good to be told the 'American system of Law is wonderful,' because that system will be used to get *you*, to silence and destroy *you*, and you might as well be a slave back in ancient Athens, who could be put to death at someone's whim."

A.&M.B.: "Do you think we will see a moral renaissance in America following in the wake of the murderous, chaotic 1960's?"

J.C.O.: "I don't see the Sixties as 'murderous and chaotic' but as part of our growth; much took place during the decade that was very, very important, but the news media concentrated, as always, upon trivial sensational events. However, one must admit that it was violent, and it was violent because there seemed no other way, through the voting booths or the courts, to make any reforms. . . . This might no longer be the case. America is not a violent nation: we just have lots of guns. Detroit, the setting of my novel, is not a city of violent, murderous people, but a city whose citizens have lots of guns. Take the guns away—distribute them to the population of London—and see what happens in London. Take the guns away,

distribute them to the population of Lisbon (where crimes of individual violence are all but unknown—but what about crimes of
political and economic violence?), and see what happens. The gun
laws should be changed, as everyone knows; they will be.

"I think there will be a gradual moral renaissance in the West—the
synthesis of the ways of Law and Love. History teaches us, in terms
of America, how wonderfully far we have come in a short span of
time, perhaps too short a span of time, considering the psychological
ill-effects of rapid change. But the FDR years, the Civil Rights years of
the Sixties, the important decisions and changes being made . . .
however gradual, and with whatever ironic side effects (men like
Governor Wallace trying to use the welfare system *against* blacks, for
instance) seem to me irrefutable landmarks of moral evolution . . .
and now the new ecological laws and bills being presented. . . . It is a
long, slow, sometimes tortuous process, becoming fully human, but
so long as we don't compare the present against some incredible
'perfection,' we are all right. People who are soured on America just
don't know enough about history; I'd advise them to take a course
in, say, German history or Russian history, or to pick up a book
about Shakespeare's London . . . or to find out what's going on
currently in some pleasant touristy place like Greece."

A.&M.B.: "Why do you feel 'the future of America will be
decided in the courtrooms rather than in the polling booths?' "

J.C.O.: "What can I say, except that it is a common delusion, to
believe (as good citizens!) that we are voting for people who will
really represent us . . . have you noticed what choices you've had?
Don't you think it's extraordinary, in a nation of millions of people,
that so few men are candidates for higher office . . . ? It isn't just in
Chicago that politics are not-to-be-believed. Changes must be made
through the courts as opposed to changes forced by street violence,
which we had in the Sixties and will probably have again, if changes
are not forthcoming!"

A.&M.B.: "You have said that you 'daydream' your stories before
setting them down. Do you ever feel, as it were, that you become a
medium?"

J.C.O.: "Most artists experience themselves as intermediaries of
one kind or another—bringing metaphors from one dimension into
another, transpersonal ideas brought into flesh, so to speak. As a Sufi

mystic says, 'The candle is not there to illuminate itself'—the artist is
not there to present himself, but to illuminate the world so far as he is
capable. However, this process of illumination—or artistic creation—is
not the exclusive possession of professional artists, but is an entirely
human activity. Everyone is an artist. Teachers, doctors, lawyers,
nurses, journalists, athletes—everyone, quite literally, when he or she
is totally immersed *in* a concentrated action that has some connection
with other people, experiences this sensation of 'egoless,' almost
mystical transport. Most people are unable to talk about it, though,
and consequently they forget it afterward. Since I am so much
absorbed in this process I experience it as an entirely natural, human
activity, a connection with higher levels of consciousness—I experience it as both a writer and a teacher."

   A.&M.B.: "You are a notably prolific writer. Have you already
embarked upon a new novel? Can you reveal its essential theme?"

   J.C.O.: "My next novel is a long complicated novel that takes
place in California—a state that is a mixture of states of the soul,
almost an entire nation in itself, a microcosm far more complex than
people think who read only the Hollywood or the atrocity stories. I
believe that out of California, out of the West, some new model of the
nation is about to flower . . . whether for good, or for good-and-evil,
who can say? That's why living now is so wonderful, a continuing
drama."

Transformation of Self: An Interview with Joyce Carol Oates

The Ohio Review/1973

From *The Ohio Review*, Autmn 1973, 50-61. © 1973 *The Ohio Review*. Reprinted by permission.

The following interview was conducted in 1972, mostly by mail.

Interviewer: Your fame is as a writer of fiction; therefore the inevitable question is: how do you view the relationship between your novels and stories and your poetry?

Oates: Everything is related. If it wouldn't alarm me, I'd someday go back through all my writing and note how the obsessions come and go, horizontally (a single psychological "plot" worked out in a story, a play, poems, parts of novels). Because these things come so directly out of my head, they go into whatever form is handy at the moment. The poems are nearly all lyric expressions of larger, dramatic, emotional predicaments, and they belong to fully-developed fictional characters who "exist" elsewhere. The poems are therefore shorthand, instantaneous, accounts of a state of mind that might have been treated in a 400-page work. I've always had a blindness for, a real inability to appreciate, the purely "lyric"—it seems so faceless, so blank and strangely inhuman, like a few bars of a Mozart symphony, perhaps the most beautiful part of the symphony but . . . but one yearns for more, to *know* more. My heroes are people like Yeats and Lawrence, who, when you read their poetry, you know are in immediate contact with an immense emotional reality. All of Yeats' poems, at least after *The Green Helmet,* are part of his life story—his personality—the Collected Works which *is* Yeats. They can be read separately, but not truly understood. And Lawrence, of course, was always writing about himself, his changing moods and ideas, so that poems like his New Mexican series relate beautifully to stories like "The Princess" or "The Woman Who Rode Away"; the poem "One

Woman to all Women" might well be spoken by Ursula of *Women In Love,* after her experience of the "glorious equilibrium" of love.

A poem of mine in *Love and Its Derangements,* called "You/Your," was written out of exactly the same maniacal stupor as certain parts of *them*; but it is from the woman's point of view, her befuddlement at her dependence upon a man, upon a man's loving *her,* from which she will get whatever identity she possesses. The woman is Jules' mistress, Nadine, who later tries to kill him. And why not? But when I wrote this part of *them* I felt Nadine to be an enemy, since I was obviously on Jules' side. In fact, many poems in *Derangements* are similar to this one—not that they belong to Nadine; they belong rather to certain experiences that gave me the material for Nadine.

Interviewer: Is this true of the title poem too?

Oates: Yes. "Love and its Derangements" is a paranoid expression of this same state of mind; it very obviously belongs to the same emotional experience as the short stories of mine "Unmailed, Unwritten Letters," "I Was in Love," sections in *Wonderland* dealing with Jesse's wife, Helene, a play I wrote recently called *Ontological Proof of My Existence,* and so forth, and so forth. This bizarre paranoia isn't anything to cultivate, but I evidently needed to write about it. Then, seeing these things externalized, out of my own imagination, they seemed to be totally foreign, freakish . . . but, like old snapshots that distort and don't flatter and yet are obviously of yourself, they must be claimed.

Interviewer: Would you, then, call this "externalization" process an aesthetic goal?

Oates: Well, here is my theory of "art," at least my temporary theory: any work can be expanded nearly to infinity, or contracted back to almost nothing. And any "work," any artistic experience, can be translated back and forth into various forms—music, painting, literature. This is possible simply because all art is dream-like, springs from the dreaming mind, and is handled either gingerly or enthusiastically by the conscious mind. You experience a certain fantasy, you can't manage it, can't comprehend it; it's a mystery; so, if you are talented in some way, you realize that you might as well try to externalize it to see if anyone else recognizes it. Art *is* communication. It's always communication, even if you, the artist, are the only one who experiences it: it's the effort of the Ego to communicate with a deeper self. Art is magnificent, divine, because it records the struggles of exceptional men to order their fantasies, their doubts, even their certainties, into an external structure that celebrates the life force itself, the energy of life, as well as the simple fact that someone created it—and especially the fact that you, the audience, are sharing it. These things are obvious, and yet profoundly important. When the work of art is tremendously effective, as *Crime and Punishment* is, it becomes to the careful reader an absolute—no, a superior—experience of its "plot," in this case mainly the committing of two murders. You never need to commit murder if you read that novel sympathetically. The redemption, the conclusion, are absolutely unconvincing; it's the committing of the murders that is important—the exorcism of "evil."

Interviewer: Well, if you could single out a particular artistic intent for your work—poetry and/or fiction—what would it be?

Oates: What I would like to do, always, in my writing is an obvious and yet perhaps audacious feat: I would like to create the psychological and emotional equivalent of an experience, so completely and in such exhaustive detail, that anyone who reads it sympathetically will have *experienced* that event in his mind (which is where we live anyway). Much of our mental life is, of course, memory. Well, I would like to have absorbed into my system certain "fictional" events so that they are as powerful as memory: so I never need to wonder, as Emma Bovary did, whether I am making a mistake or whether this is maybe a good thing. . . . I will *remember* Emma's experience and I will have learned from it. I don't really believe in "art for art's sake." All art is moral, educational, illustrative. It instructs. If it's working well, it communicates to you exactly what you'd feel if you, like Raskolnikov, had made a mistake. If it works only fitfully, feebly, it can at least tell you how boring it must be to be Samuel Beckett, and it will help you steer yourself in another direction. Even minimal art, like Kline's and Rothko's and—this is probably a terrible thing to say—Berryman's most personal poems, will make you realize how deathly, how suicidal, a certain kind of art is, this obsession with repeating a static announcement about one's own Self. My own writing is very obviously the recording of various states of mind, some of them extreme, and even a dark depressing novel like *Wonderland* can be argued to possess a certain human value: it shows you how to survive. It shows you that someone managed to get through.

Interviewer: Yes. But how do these hopes relate to the impulse toward poetry?

Oates: I believe that any truly felt lyric poem (not simply some Midwestern professor's attempt to write a Poem, to add to his bibliography for the Head of the English Department) can be expanded outward into a story—a novel—anything. Also, I believe that at any point in a lengthy work, poems can be written to very sharply illustrate what is happening, without the occasional tedium of "he walked to the door" "he said" "he smiled and wept." You do really feel a need, in a big novel—I just finished a 700-page novel yesterday—to get out from under the demands of realistic fiction, to say sharply and even bluntly what you are doing. This can be solved, of course, by going into a character's head and creating a kind of poetic-prose, using images rather than regular syntactical statements, which I do all the time.

Since the artistic impulse leaps from the unconscious mind, the form it takes in the real, shared, civilized world is really a matter of the artist's skill, his taste, his patience with his own material, and his good luck. The difference between any novel of Beckett's and any work of Chekhov's is not emotional or psychological (since their personalities are obviously similar), but a matter of the degree of formalization, of externalization, of an interior vision. Beckett gives us his thought-processes on so primary a level that they are simply language; Chekhov allows his fantasy more room, more time, chooses images in the "real," historical world to illustrate his fantasy, and therefore creates an art much more engaging than Beckett's. Beckett is deathly and boring, but not boring *because* deathly—the Death Trip can be very exciting. He's deathly because he is boring. What is the difference between Henry James and Genêt? Probably not much, primarily. If we could truly see into James' head! You can see this sort of thing beautifully in Kafka—long, sometimes-exploratory, unfinished novels; the shorter, very neat stories; the dream-fantasies he jotted down but never bothered to work up into fiction. I find the recording of the "creative process" in its bare, unadorned form less and less interesting. The dynamics of Jackson Pollock, for instance, vs. the formalized visions of Picasso, let's say some of his dancing figures. All minimal art, like Cage's music, like pop art, like the atrocious Id-pouring of much contemporary poetry, just does not interest me at all; it's only intellectual, it's sterile. "When I paint smoke," Picasso said, "I want you to be able to drive a nail in it." Exactly.

Interviewer: Your poems raise, essentially, the same issues as your fiction, but with the exception of early poems such as "Five Confessions" or "Three Dances of Death," they tend to raise those issues (bad word) in terms of *you* rather than in terms of a character. Is your poetry, then, your more "personal" medium?

Oates: Much of the poetry is indeed personal, but, then, much of the fiction is personal also; but distorted a little, made into fiction. What excites me about writing is the uses I can make of myself, of various small adventures, errors, miscalculations, stunning discoveries, near-disasters, and occasional reversals of everything, but so worked into a fictional structure that no one could guess how autobiographical it all is. Also, I like to combine myself with another person—I mean a real person—in fact, you must be cautious or I will get into you—and synthesize selves, probable experiences, etc., to make a third person, a "fictional" person. The weirdest thing I have ever done is to take a direct experience *as I was experiencing it*, second by second, and write it down, record it. This turned out to be the short story "Plot," which was published in *Paris Review* and will be in my new book of stories, *Marriages & Infidelities* (Fall 1972). The young man in the story thinks he is cracking up, totally disintegrating, and he keeps telling his readers how he feels, the pressures inside his skull, the paranoia, the half-jokes/half-pleas, and all that, and though the man is totally fiction (though based on someone I know, who had been on drugs but did recover) most of what he says I really meant. Now, when I read that story, coming across it in the library at the University of London, not expecting to see it out so soon, now, reading it is really a triumph for me, because here is this months-old self of mine, really frightened at going under, and yet thinking, imagining, that it might be just a romantic doom, and *yet* rather panicked by it. . . . And I did write it, I did record it, there it is. And here I am, a survivor. So I feel that literature is wonderfully optimistic, instructive, because it so often demonstrates how human beings get through things, maneuver themselves through chaos, and then *write about it*. I'm struck by the incredible inventive energy and craziness of someone like Bob Dylan who, in a few years, went from poverty, obscurity, maybe even ineptness, to being incredibly successful and talented, obviously a genius—a demonic genius—who then came close to total annihilation, and who *then* actually had an accident that nearly killed him, and who *then* recovered, kept going, has a family and appears to be, judging from the photographs, a totally different person. What is this? How are such bizarre things possible? Dylan went through so many transformations, emotionally and musically and *even physically*, that he must be a fictional character. But he exists, he's real. And just to exist, sometimes, can be a real triumph.

Interviewer: Is there some special attraction that the "demonic" genius holds for you?

Oates: I identify very strongly with certain highly-energetic people, like Dylan, also like Mozart, Picasso, Lawrence, Dostoyevsky, Roethke, Dickey, etc.—not because I really think I am one of them— nor do I want to patronize Dylan by this remark, because he isn't Mozart; he is much wealthier than Mozart ever was, for one thing—so far as achievement goes, but I feel a spiritual kinship. The thing about such artists is that they are so violently driven, so excited, that *what* they create is not at all important to them. Of course critics think so; critics linger lovingly over every image, every punctuation mark. But these artists are celebrating art itself, creativity itself, as it flows through their particular egos. This isn't egotism at all; it's the opposite. Picasso says somewhere that God Himself is really only "another artist." He has no fixed style but keeps "inventing" odd things, like the giraffe, the cat, the elephant, etc. He's experimental, exploratory. So this kind of artist, like "God," let's say the creative process itself, just keeps going, picking up and exploiting and dis- carding all kinds of things, imitating, borrowing, stealing, synthesizing, moving on . . . . By the time his critics figure out one thing he has done, he's jumped far ahead; he has no real interest in much of what they say; he just keeps going. Mozart had a supernatural energy, of course (and he could paint, draw, make up stories, he was marvelously talented), but he worked within a social framework, he accepted a framework, that in a way betrayed him—even though he is the greatest composer (!). Picasso, of course, broke everything down, sheer untrammelled Id combined with a shrewd, tough Ego, the makings of a real criminal or military man, and he got to be the archetype for the Artist. What he says about Art is so true that no one can really add to it: "Painting isn't an aesthetic operation, it's a form of magic designed as a mediator between the strange, hostile world and us, a way of seizing the power by giving form to our terrors as well as our desires."

That's why the whole experience is so dangerous, so alarming, when a particular self—let's say Joyce Carol Oates, of whom you are asking these questions—gets confused with the rather impersonal, inhuman flow of energy, which has nothing to do with an individual ego at all. It takes a great deal of contemplation, of near-disasters and confusions, before one realizes, as Picasso evidently did, early in his life, that there are two selves not really related, though symbiotic. All human beings are susceptible to being "used," if you want to call it that, by Nature—Nature only wants to reproduce itself. In the past a young woman like myself would simply have baby after baby, would be, simply, helplessly, a kind of machine to manufacture babies; she would have to recognize this other "self," this impersonal and rather inhuman self, that exists only to keep the species going. The artist endures some of the same perplexities. But, if he is intelligent enough, he tries to direct the fantasies, the hyperactivity, the visions and disjunctions, into external forms that can be of some aid to others; at the very least they might earn him a living. Every utterance of a private vision is a kind of achievement—even a child's finger-painting—so the utterance of a lengthy, sustained, humanly-communicating work like a novel, has got to be a real triumph. And a work of art is better than no work of art, just as something is better than nothing. Whoever said that the greatest happiness is not to have been begotten is absolutely wrong: anything is better than nothing.

Interviewer: Certainly one of the crucial differences between *Anonymous Sins* and *Love and Its Derangements* is the sense of total unity of the latter. Your first book of poems (and this is not meant in any way as a judgment), like most first books, was a collection of things, of "sins" if you will, with a mixture of temperaments and tones. And, as your title suggests, the points of view were often "anonymous." In *Love*, however, it seems to me that you've created a suite of poems, with a single tone, and a voice at once more pure and more personal, womanly. They're like the classical sonnet sequence, dedication and all, various in their dramatic and meta-phoric particulars but unified in the general thrust.

Oates: *Anonymous Sins* was written over a lengthy period of time, but *Love and Its Derangements* was written during a period of intense concentration, so that it is like a novella, the asides of a novella. However, it can't be said that the book is unified, because it is a very schizophrenic book, or one might say, less politely, it is hypocritical. It represents two different selves, two warring selves, but within one book, as if they really went together . . . but there isn't much sense of their being joined, because the one poem, the poem that brought both parts together, was of course the poem I could never write. All this sounds shadowy, unclear. But my objective, statistical, structured, "socially"-integrated self is hypocritical. This doesn't ordinarily bother me, because I don't think any way of living is perfect—to surrender totally to one's real self, like Rimbaud?—to deny one's self, like Henry James?—to compromise, as most people do? But it bothers me slightly in this case, because I believe in utter honesty in my writing (and in my teaching) and this doesn't quite make it. It's as if someone excitedly confessed to a crime, elaborately describing it, and then remarked in a footnote that the whole thing is fiction; of course; it had better be. But, perhaps, the book is of some value because it does describe how a person can evidently get along in two quite warring and distinct ways, with only a few suggestions of total disintegration (as in "Jigsaw Puzzle") but having enough wit and caution to end with a very womanly, very gentle acquiescence.

Interviewer: Your two books of poems do share, however, the preoccupation with "the imagination of pain," the metaphysics of pain. Pain seems to be the test of the authenticity of your emotion. Do you agree?

Oates: Most of my writing is preoccupied with "the imagination of pain," and this is simply because people need help with pain, never with joy. There's no need to write about happy people, happy problems; there's only the moral need to instruct readers concerning the direction to take, in order to achieve happiness (or whatever: maybe they don't want happiness, only confusion). So I feel the moral imperative to chart the psychological processes of someone, usually a hero, but sometimes a heroine, who has gone through suffering of one kind or another, but who survives it (or almost survives). I was very deeply into, very obsessed with, a certain small group of people a few years ago; they became the "Wendall" family of *them*. Well, some of these people are "real," and some fictionalized, of course, but the fact about them—which reviewers seemed never to mention, though the book was widely reviewed—is that they all survived. Critics for magazines like *Look* and *The New Yorker* dwelled on the characters' sufferings, their miseries (*them* is about poverty, in America), but what excited me about the Wendalls and what really excited them, what made them quite pleased with themselves, was how well they did. Now, of course, a well-educated, liberal, handsomely-paid New York reviewer might think that the small grubby successes of the poor all across America are depressing—and of course they would be, to such a person; but to any of the millions of "Wendalls" in the United States, these accomplishments are marvelous. My young heroine stole someone else's husband; my young hero got out of Detroit by way of a fluke, a federally-funded poverty program, and he made it to the West Coast. These are bitter little ironic successes, to us, but not to them. It takes education, money, and a lot of spare time to develop the ironic sense, the habit of irony.

Everyone experiences "pain" of one kind or another. It might be only momentary, only an idea. But there's a terrible need to suppress it, to hide it, to deny it. Therefore, we all smile at one another and assure one another that things are fine. Like Sylvia Plath near the end of her life, with what Alvarez called her "bright cheerfulness," a really American kind of hypocrisy. And it does you in, ultimately, this hypocrisy, because it cuts you off from other people who are feeling this kind of pain . . . people who might comfort you, might even save you. Therefore, unless confessional poetry is truly self-pitying and maudlin and sterile (like an academic exercise), it is quite instructive. Lowell says in the introduction to *Notebook* that there were, of course, good times for him during those combative years; but happiness somehow gets omitted. Yes, it does. It must be hinted at, however: it must be at least mentioned. When a writer fails to do this, his writing can be dangerous in proportion as it is good. Kafka is an example of this: Kafka is murderous. That's why I am so excited about Janouch's *Conversations with Kafka,* because here is the Kafka totally left out of the fiction, the letters, and the diaries. *Here* is the other half of a human being. Reading that book has been a truly exhilarating experience for me, an almost religious experience. You discover that Kafka is not murderous after all; Kafka is a saint.

As for pain in itself, however, I think it's a dead end; I think it has got to point beyond itself. In my most miserable, self-obsessed stories and poems, many of which are my best things, I attempted to get beyond the pain, somehow, simply by stating the terrible, obvious fact that in the midst of miseries, people are very often, irrationally, quite happy. This is what is so strange. You believe you can pity someone—antiseptically, safely—like a well-to-do northern liberal "pitying" the southern blacks—then you discover to your amazement and perhaps your embarrassment that these people aren't so wretched after all, but you rather thought they were, hoped they were, precisely so that you could pity them. I won't defend *Wonderland,* which is probably an immoral novel, and which I won't ever reread, myself (though I have revised the ending), but other works of mine are simply not so dark, so depressing, so joyless as some people think. It always amazes me, truly astonishes me, that critics can't see how essentially cheerful my characters are, even the vicious ones. But criminals have a right to happiness, just as much as staunch, well-educated, tax-paying reviewers and academics.

Interviewer: I wish you'd talk for a minute about some of the "formal" differences between your two volumes of poetry. Your last book feels "freer," more metaphorically aware.

Oates: The poems in *Love and Its Derangements* were worked over endlessly—revised, savagely cut, discarded and pulled back again. Each of the poems is a blur to me, a continuously shifting and changing emotional event, which is my frustration I somehow declared permanent. It was too much, the compulsion to keep rewriting, revising. And I didn't think I was aiming for "perfection," either, since I don't believe in perfection, and would be bored by it; instead, I felt that the poem would change each time I wrote it, and therefore I *must* keep rewriting it endlessly. It was as if a thousand versions of one poem clamored and demanded to be given equal utterance, equal consideration. The only thing to do, the only sane, pragmatic thing, was to force the poems into some kind of publi- cation, in the forms that seemed to work best; so there they are. My fiction comes out quite differently—it is mostly pre-imagined, pre- experienced, and I only have to record it. But the poems were not pre-existing. They had to be given a vocabulary, they had to be experienced. A third collection of my poems, *Angel Fire,* bothered

me in much the same way. I think that the writing of poetry might be
too direct for me, too troubling and explosive; I can handle fiction
better, with less after-effects. Sometimes I believe that art is cathartic,
and rids you of evils; at other times I believe it cultivates its own
tensions, and is perhaps dangerous. It's like having to paint those
canvases of Pollock's: *of course* you're going to be destroyed. Do you
create troubling works because you are troubled, or are you made
troubled by creating these works, which might be faddish, fashionable, in their morbidity? This seems to me a very interesting question.
I know that I will never write another "tragic" work, not just because it
is something of a betrayal of humanity, but because it is just too dangerous for me to live through. I feel that I touched bottom, in ways, in
Wonderland, and in some of the poems; I can glance back and say,
yes, that was it, that is going to be it; the way you might look back
over a dangerous mountain road you've travelled, rather proud at
getting through it, but really shaken, knowing you will never do it
again.

Interviewer: In both your fiction and poetry, you see love as a
violent, even destructive, experience. At one point in *Love* you speak
of being "rubbed raw with the skin/of men." Another time, in a poem
called "The Grave Dwellers," you say "we must be . . . inspired/to an
infinite love/in a series of boxes." Poe speaks of love similarly—loving
as a kind of dying. Am I reading too much into your work? Love, to
you, seems the most *self-conscious* of experiences, as we must *know*
it to *have* it.

Oates: "Love" is really two things, perhaps more. There is the
sensible, comradely, species-loving love, in which I recognize in you
and in others a humanity, a sympathetic personality, an *otherness*
that is sacred—you can even feel this in strangers, glancing at
strangers riding by on a bus (just a meeting of eyes, thank God, and
then they're gone). Then there is the totally irrational, possessive,
ego-destroying love, which can't be controlled and is, perhaps, a
pathological condition of the soul. These two emotions have nothing
in common; except, perhaps, the first can grow out of the second, as
when people fall in love, become acquainted and then marry. And
hope it will endure. I can't begin to explain the second kind of "love."
It is truly bizarre, mysterious, anti-social. It is even in a way anti-
natural, anti-species, because it sometimes generates in one person

(usually the man) a desire to kill the beloved, if the beloved can't be captured. What can one do, how can one escape this? It's like a free-floating germ, a kind of virus for which there is no cure. I just finished a long novel, called *Do With Me What You Will*, which is mainly about the experience of this kind of love, how it is endured, and finally shaped into something civilized—"marriage"—but at great cost to the lovers and to other people. It is so essentially murderous, that someone must be a victim; if not the lovers, then innocent by-standers. But what solution is there? Bad as it is to fall hopelessly in love with someone unattainable (one could at least write infinite variations on a love poem, like Yeats to Maud Gonne), it is far worse to be the innocent object of someone's (unattainable) love. Then you feel yourself hunted, boxed-up, continually *thought about*; you realize that you are part of someone's fantasy, uncontrollable by himself or by you, and this is truly terrifying. But if the woman, the "beloved object," halfway shares in the obsession, then she enters a hellish experience in which she struggles to be free and/but also to perpetuate the delusion, which is so pleasant. It is a kind of madness, obviously, in which both lovers are very energetic and creative—in the artistic sense, really—because they create together a kind of manic fiction, prose or poetry, that they may have to abandon sooner or later, but which they will never forget. And to have gone through it, this is quite an accomplishment also; this is not exactly a negligible feat.

Joyce Carol Oates

Judith Applebaum/1978

From *Publisher's Weekly*, 26 June 1978, 12-13. © 1978 Xerox Corporation. Reprinted by permission.

Sure enough, the face is familiar. From the jackets of book after book, from the December 1972 *Newsweek* cover story, from the journalists' interviews that appear from time to time where Joyce Carol Oates teaches or gives poetry readings, her dark hair, thin features and outsize eyes have come to be readily recognizable. But what no picture can convey—as we discovered when Oates dropped in at *PW*'s office one afternoon not long ago—is the intensely sensuous quality of her presence.

Even a few minutes of conversation suffice to create the impression of a creature equipped with antennae that continually scan the environment, not in the interests of self-preservation, like some watchful, anxious animal, or in the dutiful, mechanized manner of radar, but rather as if all the world knew an alert observer would be rewarded with flashes of illumination.

Given this magnitude of attention, it is not surprising that Oates has achieved a number of literary distinctions (she was elected to membership in the American Academy and Institute of Arts and Letters in May of this year, and she's won the National Book Award— for *them* in 1970). And it fits, too, that she has become one of today's most prolific writers—to the point, in fact, where she apparently feels impelled to adopt a slightly defensive posture about the volume of novels, short stories, essays and poems she turns out. ("In the past," she once told an interviewer, even "people who were in physical pain, who were not very well, like Sir Walter Scott and a number of others, just kept on working. D. H. Lawrence was never really well, and he wrote prodigiously. He hiked across Europe. And he was writing all the time—and nobody told him that he was too prolific. We live in a time where weakness is falsely extolled, as if it were sensitivity," she went on, concluding, "I don't think it is.")

Books by Joyce Carol Oates fill a column in the current Books in

Print, but it was her latest novel—*Son of the Morning*—that she most wanted to talk about. The book, she told us, her voice soft, her words flowing evenly, without interruption, was "a very mesmerizing novel to write." *Son of the Morning* tells the story of Nathanael Vickery, who experiences "seven revelations of extraordinary magnitude; seven times when God seizes him in the flesh," and is compelled, by his intimate relationship with God, to save souls in the United States of the mid-20th century (*PW* Forecasts, June 19).

"I wanted to write about religious experience from the other side, about interior experience," Oates explained. "I've been interested in it for many years, and I think religious experience is real and possible to everyone. Also, I am very interested in the '60s and '70s phenomena of religious revival in America."

Believing that religion "becomes fossilized when it's put into an exterior form," Oates aims to show in her new book "how interior experience becomes modified and can't be controlled as it is taken over by the evangelical church." Many young people are "extremely susceptible" to this kind of religion today, said Joyce Carol Oates with compassion, "because they don't have any other beliefs."

While working on *Son of the Morning*, Oates devoted hours each day to reading the Bible. "I wanted to put myself in the place of a fundamentalist Protestant who could go to the Bible every day for guidance and would not have any critical or historical preconceptions," she said, adding that "getting into that frame of mind was a very shattering experience."

"The world of the Bible is a world of intense drama," she went on, speaking quickly and with marked conviction. "Every day is a battle between good and evil, between God and the Devil. I spent many hours last year in that world, like Nathan, like my hero. You get so caught up in it you feel that in just a few minutes there will be a revelation."

When her new book appears next month, it will join 20 other Joyce Carol Oates titles on the list of the small New York publishing firm called Vanguard Press, Inc., which Oates first approached when she was still in college and has stayed with ever since. ("I read in a magazine that Vanguard was interested in young writers, so I sent them a manuscript and they wrote a friendly letter and said they were very interested in seeing more of my work, so when I had another manuscript I sent that and they published it.")

Oates speaks well of Vanguard and of the three other publishers who regularly issue her work: Fawcett, for paperback reprints; Louisiana State University Press, for several volumes of poetry; and Black Sparrow, for "more experimental" prose and some poems in limited editions. (Black Sparrow added Joyce Carol Oates to its list when its president and editor, John Martin, wrote to tell her he admired an essay she'd written about D. H. Lawrence and to ask whether he could publish it in booklet form. "I said, 'Of course,' " Oates reports, "he made a very handsome little book, and we became friendly through the mail.")

Asked about her teaching experience, she responds thoughtfully, volunteering that she will be a writer in residence at Princeton during the coming academic year while on leave from the University of Windsor in Ontario (where both she and her husband, Raymond Smith, are members of the English department). Her main task with her students, she says, is to "make them understand that you have to be patient. I give them examples of great writers who took a long time to mature. The secret is to keep going—not to give up. There's an analogy between music and writing," she adds, eyes searching some far horizon for the key to the process she's describing. "I take piano lessons, and the early stages with a new piece are stumbling and disheartening. But if you keep on, it's incredible how you can build skills, how something clicks."

Still, it's *Son of the Morning* that seems to engage Oates's attention most fully just now. Like *The Assassins* (1975) and *Wonderland* (1971), *Son of the Morning* "disturbed me very much," she says. "When I got done with each of them I vowed I'd never do anything like that again. I think I'm going to do some lighter work now. I'm working on some short stories. I participated in the recent U.S.-Soviet writers conference and I'm reading Soviet writers." Then, pausing, seeming to monitor some play of inner urgencies, she carefully presents her findings: "I was greatly relieved when I finished the book. I told myself I wouldn't write anything quite so intense for a while. But I probably will write some more about religious experience, because I haven't fully explored it yet."

Joyce Carol Oates: The Art of Fiction LXXII
Robert Phillips/1978

From *The Paris Review*, Fall 1978, 199-206. © 1978 Robert Phillips. Reprinted by permission.

Joyce Carol Oates is the rarest of commodities, an author modest about her work, though there is such a quantity of it that she has three publishers—one for fiction, one for poetry, and a "small press" for more experimental work, limited editions and books her other publishers simply can not schedule.

In the fall of 1978, Ms. Oates and her professor-husband, Raymond Smith, moved from the University of Windsor in Canada, to New Jersey, where she assumed duties as writer-in-residence at Princeton University. Despite the demands of her students and writing, she continues to devote much energy to *The Ontario Review*, a literary quarterly which her husband edits and for which she serves as a contributing editor.

Ms. Oates is striking looking, slender with straight dark hair and large, inquiring eyes. A highly attractive woman, she is not photogenic; no photo has ever done justice to her appearance, which conveys grace and high intelligence. If her manner is taken for aloofness—as it sometimes has been—it is, in fact, a shyness which the publication of thirty-three books, the production of three plays, and the winning of the National Book Award for the novel, *them,* has not displaced.

Anyone who has known her for a long time, however, is likely to point out how less shy she is than formerly. As an undergraduate at Syracuse University, where she was valedictorian of a class of over 2,000—receiving an "A" in all subjects but physical education—she was too timid to read her papers aloud when called upon in class. Professors read them for her.

This interview began at the Windsor home in the summer of 1976. When interviewed her speaking voice was, as always, soft and reflective. One receives the impression she never speaks in anything but perfectly-formed sentences. Ms. Oates answered all questions openly, while

curled with her Persian cats upon a sofa. (She is a confirmed cat-lover and recently took in two more kittens at
the Princeton house.) Talk continued during a stroll by the
bank of the Detroit river where she confessed to having sat
for hours, watching the horizon, the boats and dreaming
her characters into existence. She sets these dreams physically onto paper on a writing table in one corner of the
master bedroom.

Additional questions were asked in New York during the
1976 Christmas season when Ms. Oates and her husband
attended a seminar on her work which was part of that
year's Modern Language Association convention. Many of
the questions in this interview were answered via correspondence. She felt only by writing out her replies could
she say precisely what she wished to, without possibility of
misunderstanding or misquotation.

Interviewer: We may as well get this one over with first: You're
frequently charged with producing too much.

Oates: Productivity is a relative matter. And it's really insignificant:
What is ultimately important is a writer's strongest books. It may be
the case that we all must write many books in order to achieve a few
lasting ones—just as a young writer or poet might have to write hundreds of poems before writing his first significant one. Each book as it
is written, however, is a completely absorbing experience, and feels
always as if it were *the* work I was born to write. Afterward, of course,
as the years pass, it's possible to become more detached, more
critical.

I really don't know what to say. I note and can to some extent
sympathize with the objurgatory tone of certain critics who feel that I
write too much because, quite wrongly, they believe they ought to
have read most of my books before attempting to criticize a recently-
published one. (At least I *think* that's why they react a bit irritably.)
Yet each book is a world unto itself, and must stand alone and it
should not matter whether a book is a writer's first, or tenth, or
fiftieth.

Interviewer: About your critics—do you read them, usually?
Have you ever learned anything from a book review or an essay on
your work?

Oates: Sometimes I read reviews, and without exception I will read critical essays that are sent to me. The critical essays are interesting on their own terms. Of course it's a pleasure simply to discover that someone has read and responded to one's work; being understood, and being praised, is beyond expectation most of the time. . . . The average review is a quickly-written piece not meant to be definitive. So it would be misguided for a writer to read such reviews attentively. All writers without exception find themselves clapperclawed from time to time; I think the experience (provided one survives it) is wonderfully liberating: After the first death there is no other. . . . A writer who has published as many books as I have, has developed, of necessity, a hide like a rhino's, while inside there dwells a frail, hopeful butterfly of a spirit.

Interviewer: Returning to the matter of your "productivity": Have you ever dictated into a machine?

Oates: No, oddly enough I've written my last several novels in long-hand first. I had an enormous, rather frightening stack of pages and notes for *The Assassins,* probably 800 pages—or was it closer to 1000? It alarms me to remember. *Childwold* needed to be written in long-hand, of course. And now everything finds its initial expression in long-hand and the typewriter has become a rather alien thing—a thing of formality and impersonality. My first novels were all written on a typewriter: first draft straight through, then revisions, then final draft. But I can't do that any longer.

The thought of dictating into a machine doesn't appeal to me at all. Henry James's later works would have been better had he resisted that curious sort of self-indulgence, dictating to a secretary. The roaming garrulousness of ordinary speech is usually corrected when it's transcribed into written prose.

Interviewer: Do you ever worry—considering the vast body of your work—if you haven't written a particular scene before, or had characters say the same lines?

Oates: Evidently there are writers (John Cheever, Mavis Gallant come immediately to mind) who never reread their work, and there are others who reread constantly. I suspect I am somewhere in the middle. If I thought I *had* written a scene before, or written the same lines before, I would simply look it up.

Interviewer: What kind of work schedule do you follow?

Oates: I haven't any formal schedule, but I love to write in the morning before breakfast. Sometimes the writing goes so smoothly that I don't take a break for many hours—and consequently have breakfast at two or three in the afternoon on good days. On school days, days that I teach, I usually write for an hour or forty-five minutes in the morning, before my first class. But I don't have any formal schedule and at the moment I am feeling rather melancholy, or derailed, or simply lost, because I completed a novel some weeks ago and haven't begun another . . . except in scattered, stray notes.

Interviewer: Do you find emotional stability is necessary in order to write? Or can you get to work whatever your state of mind? Is your mood reflected in what you write? How do you describe that perfect state in which you can write from early morning into the afternoon?

Oates: One must be pitiless about this matter of 'mood.' In a sense the writing will *create* the mood. If art is, as I believe it to be, a genuinely transcendental function—a means by which we rise out of limited, parochial states of mind—then it should not matter very much what states of mind or emotion we are in. Generally I've found this to be true: I have forced myself to begin writing when I've been utterly exhausted, when I've felt my soul as thin as a playing-card, when nothing has seemed worth enduring for another five minutes . . . and somehow the activity of writing changes everything. Or appears to do so. Joyce said of the underlying structure of *Ulysses*—the Odyssean parallel and parody—that he really didn't care whether it was plausible, so long as it served as a bridge to get his 'soldiers' across. Once they were across, what does it matter if the bridge collapses? One might say the same thing about the use of one's self as a means for the writing to get written. Once the soldiers are across the stream. . . .

Interviewer: What does happen when you finish a novel? Is the next project one that has been waiting in line? Or is the choice more spontaneous?

Oates: When I complete a novel I set it aside, and begin work on short stories, and eventually another long work. When I complete *that* novel I return to the earlier novel and rewrite much of it. In the meantime the second novel lies in a desk drawer. Sometimes I work on two novels simultaneously, though one usually forces the other into the background. The rhythm of writing, revising, writing, revising, etc., seems to suit me. I am inclined to think that as I grow older I will come to be infatuated with the art of revision, and there may come a time when I will dread giving up a novel at all. My next novel, *Unholy Loves,* was written around the time of *Childwold,* for instance, and revised after the completion of that novel, and again revised this past spring and summer. My reputation for writing quickly and effortlessly notwithstanding, I am strongly in favor of intelligent, even fastidious revision, which is, or certainly should be, an art in itself.

Interviewer: Do you keep a diary?

Oates: I began keeping a formal journal several years ago. It resembles a sort of on-going letter to myself, mainly about literary matters. What interests me in the process of my own experience is the wide range of my feelings. For instance, after I finish a novel I tend to think of the experience of having written it as being largely pleasant and challenging. But in fact (for I keep careful records) the experience is various: I do suffer temporary bouts of frustration and inertia and depression. There are pages in recent novels that I've rewritten as many as 17 times, and a story, "The Widows," which I revised both before and after publication in *The Hudson Review,* and then revised slightly again before I included it in my next collection of stories—a fastidiousness that could go on into infinity.

Afterward, however, I simply forget. My feelings crystallize (or are mythologized) into something much less complex. All of us who keep journals do so for different reasons I suppose, but we must have in common a fascination with the surprising patterns that emerge over the years—a sort of arabesque in which certain elements appear and reappear, like the designs in a well-wrought novel. The voice of my journal is very much like the one I find myself using in these replies to you: the voice in which I think or meditate when I'm not writing fiction.

Interviewer: Besides writing and teaching, what daily special activities are important to you? Travel, jogging, music? I hear you're an excellent pianist?

Oates: We travel a great deal, usually by car. We've driven slowly across the continent several times, and we've explored the South and New England and of course New York State with loving thoroughness. As a pianist I've defined myself as an "enthusiastic amateur," which is about the most merciful thing that can be said. I like to draw; I like to listen to music, and I spend an inordinate amount of time doing nothing. I don't even think it can be called day-dreaming.

I also enjoy that much-maligned occupation of housewifery, but hardly dare say so, things being what they are today. I like to cook, to tend plants, to garden (minimally), to do simple domestic things, to stroll around shopping malls and observe the qualities of people, overhearing snatches of conversations, noting people's appearances, their clothes, and so forth. Walking and driving a car are part of my life as a writer, really. I can't imagine myself apart from these activities.

Interviewer: Despite critical and financial success, you continue to teach. Why?

Oates: I teach a full load at the University of Windsor, which means three courses. One is creative writing, one is the graduate seminar (in the Modern Period), the third is an oversized (115 students) undergraduate course that is lively and stimulating but really too swollen to be satisfying to me. There is, generally, a closeness between students and faculty at Windsor that is very rewarding, however. Anyone who teaches knows that you don't *really* experience a text until you've taught it, in loving detail, with an intelligent and responsive class. At the present time I'm going through Joyce's work with nine graduate students and each seminar meeting is very exciting (and draining) and I can't think, frankly, of anything else I would rather do.

Interviewer: It is a sometimes-publicized fact that your professor-husband does not read most of your work. Is there any practical reason for this?

Oates: Ray has such a busy life of his own, preparing classes, editing *The Ontario Review* and so forth, that he really hasn't time to read my work. I do, occasionally, show him reviews and he makes brief comments on them. I would have liked, I think, to have established an easy-going relationship with some other writers, but somehow that never came about. Two or three of us at Windsor do read one another's poems, but criticism as such is minimal. I've never been able to respond very fully to criticism, frankly, because I've usually been absorbed in another work by the time the criticism is available to me. Also, critics sometimes appear to be addressing themselves to works other than those I remember writing.

Interviewer: Do you feel in any way an expatriate or an exile, living in Canada?

Oates: We are certainly exiles of a sort. But we would be, I think, exiles if we lived in Detroit as well. Fortunately, Windsor is really an international, cosmopolitan community and our Canadian colleagues are not intensely and narrowly nationalistic.

But I wonder—doesn't everyone feel rather exiled? When I return home to Millerport, New York, and visit nearby Lockport, the extra-ordinary changes that have taken place make me feel like a stranger; the mere passage of time makes us all exiles. The situation is a comic one, perhaps, since it affirms the power of the evolving community over the individual, but I think we tend to feel it as tragic. Windsor is a relatively stable community, and my husband and I have come to feel, oddly, more at home here than we probably would anywhere else.

Interviewer: Have you ever consciously changed your life style to help your work as a writer?

Oates: Not really. My nature is orderly and observant and scrup-ulous, and deeply introverted, so life wherever I attempt it turns out to be claustral. *Live like the bourgeois,* Flaubert suggested, but I was living like that long before I came across Flaubert's remark.

Interviewer: You wrote *Do With Me What You Will* during your year living in London. While there you met many writers such as Doris Lessing, Margaret Drabble, Colin Wilson, Iris Murdoch—writers you respect, as your reviews of their work indicates. Would you make any observations on the role of the writer in society in England versus that which you experience here?

Oates: The English novelist is almost without exception an observer of society. (I suppose I mean "society" in its most immed-iate, limited sense.) Apart from writers like Lawrence (who doesn't seem altogether *English,* in fact) there hasn't been an intense interest in subjectivity, in the psychology of living, breathing human beings. Of course there have been marvelous novels. And there *is* Doris Lessing, who writes books that can no longer be categorized: fictional parable, autobiography, allegory . . . ? And John Fowles. And Iris Murdoch.

But there is a feel to the American novel that is radically different. We are willing to risk being called "formless" by people whose ideas of form are rigidly limited, and we are wilder, more exploratory, more ambitious, perhaps less easily shamed, less easily discouraged. The intellectual life as such we tend to keep out of our novels, fearing the sort of highly readable but ultimately disappointing cerebral quality of Huxley's work . . . or, on a somewhat lower level, C. P. Snow's.

Interviewer: The English edition of *Wonderland* has a different ending from the American. Why? Do you often rewrite published work?

Oates: I was forced to rewrite the ending of that particular novel because it struck me that the first ending was not the correct one. I have not rewritten any other published work (except of course for short stories, which sometimes get rewritten before inclusion in a book) and don't intend to if I can possibly help it.

Interviewer: You've written novels on highly specialized fields, such as brain surgery. How do you research such backgrounds?

Oates: A great deal of reading, mainly. Some years ago I developed a few odd symptoms that necessitated my seeing a doctor, and since there was for a time talk of my being sent to a neurologist, I nervously and superstitiously began reading the relevant journals. What I came upon so chilled me that I must have gotten well as a result . . .

Interviewer: In addition to the novel about medicine, you've written one each on law, politics, religion, spectator sports: Are you consciously filling out a "program" of novels about American life?

Oates: Not really consciously. The great concern with "medicine" really grew out of an experience of some duration that brought me into contact with certain thoughts of mortality: of hospitals, illnesses, doctors, the world of death and dying and our human defenses against such phenomena. (A member of my family to whom I was very close died rather slowly of cancer.) I attempted to deal with my own very inchoate feelings about these matters by dramatizing what I saw to be contemporary responses to "mortality." My effort to wed myself with a fictional character and our synthesis in turn with a larger, almost allegorical condition resulted in a novel that was difficult to write and also, I suspect, difficult to read.

A concern with law seemed to spring naturally out of the thinking many of us were doing in the '60s: what is the relationship between "law" and civilization, what hope has civilization without "law," and yet what hope has civilization *with* law as it has developed in our tradition? More personal matters blended with the larger issues of "crime" and "guilt" so that I felt I was able to transcend a purely private and purely local drama that might have had emotional significance for me, but very little beyond that; quite by accident I found myself writing about a woman conditioned to be unnaturally "passive" in a world of hearty masculine combat—an issue that became topical even as the novel *Do With Me What You Will* was published, and is topical still, to some extent.

The "political" novel, *The Assassins,* grew out of two experiences I had some years ago, at high-level conferences involving politicians, academic specialists, lawyers, and a scattering—no, hardly that—of literary people. (I won't be more specific at the moment.) A certain vertiginous fascination with work which I noted in my own nature I was able to objectify (and, I think, exaggerate) in terms of the various characters' fanaticism involving their own "work"—most obviously in Andrew Petrie's obsession with "transforming the consciousness of America." *The Assassins* is about megalomania and its inevitable consequences and it seemed necessary that the assassins be involved in politics, given the peculiar conditions of our era.

The new "religious" novel, *Son of the Morning,* is rather painfully autobiographical, in part; but only in part. The religion it explores is not institutional but rather subjective, intensely personal, so as a novel it is perhaps not like the earlier three I have mentioned, or the racing novel, *With Shuddering Fall.* Rather, *Son of the Morning* is a novel that begins with wide ambitions and ends very, very humbly.

Interviewer: Somewhere in print you called *The Assassins* the favorite of your novels. It received very mixed reviews. I've often thought that book was misread. For instance, I think the "martyr" in that novel arranged for his own assassination, true? And that his wife was never really attacked outside the country house; she never left it. Her maiming was all confined within her head.

Oates: What a fine surprise! You read the scene exactly as it was meant to be read. Even well-intentioned reviewers missed the point; so far as I know, only two or three people read Yvonne's scene as I had intended it to be read. Yet the hallucinatory nature of the "dismemberment" scene is explicit. And Andrew Petrie did, of course, arrange for his own assassination, as the novel makes clear in its concluding pages.

The novel has been misread, of course, partly because it's rather long and I think reviewers, who are usually pressed for time, simply treated it in a perfunctory way. I'm not certain that it is my favorite novel. But it is, or was, my most ambitious. It involved a great deal of effort, the collating of passages (and memories) that differ from or contradict one another. One becomes attached to such perverse, maddening ugly ducklings, but I can't really blame reviewers for being impatient with the novel. As my novels grow in complexity they please me more and please the "literary world" hardly at all—a sad situation, but not a paralyzing one.

Interviewer: It's not merely a matter of complexity. One feels that your fiction has become more and more urgent, more subjective and less concerned with the outward details of this world—especially in *Childwold*. Was that novel a deliberate attempt to write a "poetic novel"? Or is it a long poem?

Oates: I don't see that *Childwold* is not concerned with the out-ward details of the world. In fact it's made up almost entirely of visual details—of the natural world, of the farm the Bartletts own, and of the small city they gravitate to. But you are right, certainly, in suggesting that it is a "poetic novel." I had wanted to create a prose poem in the form of a novel, or a novel in the form of a prose poem: the exciting thing for me was to deal with the tension that arose between the image-centered structure of poetry and the narrative-centered and linear structure of the interplay of persons that constitutes a novel. In other words, poetry focuses upon the image, the particular thing, or emotion, or feeling; while prose fiction focuses upon motion through time and space. The one impulse is toward stasis, the other toward movement. Between the two impulses there arose a certain tension that made the writing of the novel quite challenging. I suppose it is an experimental work but I shy away from thinking of my work in those terms: it seems to me there is a certain self-consciousness about anyone who sets himself up as an 'experimental' writer. All writing is experimental.

But experimentation for its own sake doesn't much interest me; it seems to belong to the early '60's, when Dadaism was being rediscovered. In a sense we are all post-*Wake* writers and it's Joyce, and only Joyce, who casts a long terrifying shadow. . . . The problem is that virtuoso writing appeals to the intellect and tends to leave one's emotions untouched. When I read aloud to my students the last few pages of *Finnegan's Wake,* and come to that glorious, and heartbreaking, final section ("But you're changing, acoolsha, you're changing from me, I can feel.") I think I'm able to communicate the almost overwhelmingly beautiful emotion behind it, and the experience certainly leaves *me* shaken, but it would be foolish to think that the average reader, even the average intelligent reader, would be willing to labor at the *Wake,* through those hundreds of dense pages, in order to attain an emotional and spiritual sense of the work's wholeness, as well as its genius. Joyce's *Ulysses* appeals to me more: that graceful synthesis of the "naturalistic" and the "symbolic" suits my temperament also. . . . I try to write books that can be read in one way by a literal-minded reader, and in quite another way by a reader alert to symbolic abbreviation and parodistic elements. And yet, it's the same book—or nearly. A trompe l'oeil, a work of *as if.*

Interviewer: Very little has been made of the humor in your work, the parody. Some of your books, like *Expensive People, The Hungry Ghosts,* and parts of *Wonderland* seem almost Pinteresque in their absurd humor. Is Pinter an influence? Do you consider yourself a Comedic writer?

Oates: There's been humor of a sort in my writing from the first; but it's understated, or deadpan. Pinter has never struck me as very funny. Doesn't he really write tragedy?

I liked Ionesco at one time. And Kafka. And Dickens (from whom Kafka learned certain effect, though he uses them, of course, for different ends). I respond to English satire, as I mentioned earlier. Absurdist or "dark" or "black" or whatever: what isn't tragic belongs to the comic spirit. The novel is nourished by both and swallows both up greedily.

Interviewer: What have you learned from Kafka?

Oates: To make a jest of the horror. To take myself less seriously.

Interviewer: John Updike has been accused of a lack of violence in his work. You're often accused of portraying too much. What is the function of violence in your work?

Oates: Given the number of pages I have written, and the "violent" incidents dispersed throughout them, I rather doubt that I am a violent writer in any meaningful sense of the word. Certainly the violence is minimal in a novel like *them,* which purported to be a naturalistic work set in Detroit in the '60's; real life is much more chaotic.

Interviewer: Which of your books gave you the greatest trouble to write? And which gave the greatest pleasure or pride.

Oates: Both *Wonderland* and *The Assassins* were difficult to write. *Expensive People* was the least difficult. I am personally very fond of *Childwold* since it represents, in a kind of diffracted way, a complete world made of money and imagination, a blending-together of different times. It always surprises me that other people find that novel admirable because, to me, it seems very private . . . the sort of thing a writer can do only once.

Aside from that, *Do With Me What You Will* gives me a fair amount of pleasure, and of course, I am closest to the novel I finished most recently, *Son of the Morning.* (In general I think we are always fondest of the books we've just completed, aren't we? For obvious reasons.) But when I think of Jules and Maureen and Loretta of *them* and I wonder if perhaps that isn't my favorite novel, after all.

Interviewer: For whom do you write—yourself, your friends, your "public"? Do you imagine an ideal reader for your work?

Oates: Well, there are certain stories, like those in *The Hungry Ghosts,* which I have written for an academic community and, in some cases, for specific people. But in general the writing writes itself—I mean a character determines his or her "voice" and I must follow along. Had I my own way the first section of *The Assassins* would be much abbreviated. But it was impossible to shut Hugh Petrie up once he got going and, long and painful and unwieldy as his section is, it's nevertheless been shortened. The problem with creating such highly conscious and intuitive characters is that they tend to perceive the contours of the literary landscape in which they dwell and, like Kasch of *Childwold,* try to guide or even to take over the direction of the narrative. Hugh did not want to die, and so his section went on and on, and it isn't an exaggeration to say that I felt real dismay in dealing with him.

Son of the Morning is a first-person narration by a man who is addressing himself throughout to God. Hence the whole novel is a

prayer. Hence the ideal reader is, then, God. Everyone else, myself
included, is secondary.

Interviewer: Do you consider yourself religious? Do you feel
there is a firm religious basis to your work?

Oates: I wish I knew how to answer this. Having completed a
novel that is saturated with what Jung calls the God-experience, I find
that I know less than ever about myself and my own beliefs. I have
beliefs, of course, like everyone—but I don't always believe in them.
Faith comes and goes. God diffracts into a bewildering plenitude of
elements—the environment, love, friends and family, career, profession, "fate," biochemical harmony or disharmony, whether the sky is
slate-gray or a bright mesmerizing blue. These elements then coa-
lesce again into something seemingly unified. But it's a human
predilection, isn't it?—our tendency to see, and to wish to see, what
we've projected outward upon the universe from our own souls? I
hope to continue to write about religious experience, but at the
moment I feel quite drained, quite depleted. And as baffled as ever.

Interviewer: You mention Jung. Is Freud also an influence?
Laing?

Oates: Freud I have always found rather limited and biased; Jung
and Laing I've read only in recent years. As an undergraduate at
Syracuse University I discovered Nietzsche and it may be the
Nietzschean influence (which is certainly far more provocative than
Freud's) that characterizes some of my work. I don't really know,
consciously. For me, stories usually begin—or began, since I write so
few of them now—out of some magical association between characters and their settings. There are some stories (I won't say which
ones) which evolved almost entirely out of their settings, usually rural.

Interviewer: Your earliest stories and novels seem influenced by
Faulkner and by Flannery O'Connor. Are these influences you
acknowledge? Are there others?

Oates: I've been reading for so many years, and my influences
must be so vast—it would be very difficult to answer. An influence I
rarely mention is Thoreau, whom I read at a very impressionable age,
(my early teens), and Henry James, O'Connor and Faulkner,
certainly, Katherine Anne Porter, and Dostoyevsky. An odd mixture.

Interviewer: The title *Wonderland,* and frequent other allusions in your work, point toward a knowledge of, if not an affinity for, Lewis Carroll. What is the connection, and is it an important one?

Oates: Lewis Carroll's *Alice in Wonderland* and *Through the Looking-glass* were my very first books. Carroll's wonderful blend of illogic and humor and horror and justice has always appealed to me, and I had a marvelous time teaching the books last year in my undergraduate course.

Interviewer: Was there anything you were particularly afraid of, as a child?

Oates: Like most children, I was probably afraid of a variety of things. The unknown? The possibility of those queer fortuitous metamorphoses that seem to overtake certain of Carroll's characters? Physical pain? Getting lost? . . . My proclivity for the irreverent and the nonsensical was either inspired by Carroll, or confirmed by him. I was always, and continue to be, an essentially mischievous child. This is one of my best-kept secrets.

Interviewer: You began writing at a very early age. Was it encouraged by your family? Was yours a family of artistic ambitions?

Oates: In later years my parents have become "artistic," but when they were younger, and their children were younger, they had no time for anything much except work. I was always encouraged by my parents, my grandmother, and my teachers, to be creative. I can't remember when I first began to tell stories—by drawing, it was then—but I must have been very young. It was an instinct I followed quite naturally.

Interviewer: Much of your work is set in the 1930s, a period during which you were merely an infant at best. Why is that decade so important to your work or vision?

Oates: Since I was born in 1938, the decade is of great significance to me. This was the world of my parents, who were young adults at the time, the world I was born into. The '30s seem in an odd way still "living" to me, partly in terms of my parents' and grandparents' memories, and partly in terms of its treatment in books and films. But the '20s is too remote—lost to me entirely! I simply haven't had the imaginative power to get that far back.

I identify very closely with my parents in ways I can't satisfactorily explain. The lives they lived before I was born seem somehow accessible to me. Not directly, of course, but imaginatively. A memory belonging to my mother or father seems almost to "belong" to me. In studying old photographs I am struck sometimes by a sense of my being contemporary with my parents—as if I'd known them when they were, let's say, only teenagers. Is this odd? I wonder. I rather suspect others share in their family's experiences and memories without knowing quite how.

Interviewer: When we were undergraduates together at Syracuse, you already were something of a legend. It was rumored you'd finish a novel, turn it over, and immediately begin writing another on the backside. When both sides were covered, you'd throw it all out, and reach for clean paper. Was it at Syracuse you first became aware you were going to be a writer?

Oates: I began writing in high school, consciously training myself by writing novel after novel and always throwing them out when I completed them. I remember a 300-page book of interrelated stories that must have been modeled on Hemingway's *In Our Time* (I hadn't yet read *Dubliners*,) though the subject matter was much more romantic than Hemingway's. I remember a bloated trifurcated novel that had as its vague model *The Sound and the Fury* . . . Fortunately these experiments were thrown away and I haven't remembered them until this moment.

Syracuse was a very exciting place academically and intellectually for me. I doubt that I missed more than half a dozen classes in my four years there; and none of them in English.

Interviewer: I remember you were in a sorority. It is incredible to contemplate you as "a sorority girl."

Oates: My experience in a sorority wasn't disastrous, but merely despairing. (I tried to resign but found out that upon joining I had signed some sort of legal contract.) However, I did make some close friends in the sorority, so the experience wasn't a total loss. I would never do it again, certainly. In fact, it's one of the three or four things in my entire life I would never do again.

Interviewer: Why was life in a Syracuse sorority so despairing? Have you written about it?

Oates: The racial and religious bigotry; the asininity of 'secret ceremonies'; the moronic emphasis upon 'activities' totally unrelated to—in fact antithetical to—intellectual exploration; the bullying of the presumably weak by the presumably strong; the deliberate pursuit of an attractive 'image' for the group as a whole, no matter how cynical the individuals might have been; the aping of the worst American traits—boosterism, God-fearing-ism, smug ignorance, a craven worship of conformity; the sheer *mess* of the place once one got beyond the downstairs. . . . I tried to escape in my junior year but a connection between sororities and the Dean of Women and the university housing office made escape all but impossible, and it seemed that, in my freshman naïveté, I had actually signed some sort of contract that had 'legal' status . . . all of which quite cowed me. I remember a powdered and perfumed alum explaining the sorority's exclusion of Jews and blacks: "You see, we have conferences at the Lake Placid Club, and wouldn't it be a shame if *all* our members couldn't attend. . . . Why, it would be embarrassing for them, wouldn't it?"

I was valedictorian of my class, the class of 1960. I fantasized beginning my address by saying: "I managed to do well academically at Syracuse despite the concerted efforts of my sorority to prevent me. . . . "

I haven't written about it, and never will. It's simply too stupid and trivial a subject. To even *care* about such adolescent nonsense one would have to have the sensitivity of a John O'Hara, who seems to have taken it all seriously.

Interviewer: I recall you won the poetry contest at Syracuse in your senior year. But your books of poetry appeared relatively later than your fiction. Were you always writing poetry?

Oates: No, I really began to write poetry later. The poetry still comes with difficulty, I must admit. Tiny lyric asides, droll wry enigmatic statements: they aren't easy, are they? I'm assembling a book which I think will be my last—of poems, I mean. No one wants to read a novelist's poetry. It's enough—too much, in fact—to deal with the novels. Strangely enough my fellow poets have been magnanimous indeed in accepting me as a poet. I would not have been surprised had they ignored me, but, in fact, they've been wonderfully supportive and encouraging. Which contradicts the general notion that poets are highly competitive and jealous of one another's accomplishments . . .

Interviewer: You say no one wants to read a novelist's poetry.

What about Robert Penn Warren? John Updike? Erica Jong? I
suppose Allen Tate and James Dickey are poets who happened to
write novels . . .

Oates: I suppose I was thinking only of hypothetical reactions to
my own poetry. Robert Penn Warren aside, however, there *is* a
tendency on the part of critics to want very much to categorize
writers. Hence one is either a writer of prose or of poetry. If Lawrence
hadn't written those novels he would have been far more readily
acclaimed as one of the greatest poets in the language. As it is,
however, his poetry has been neglected. (At least until recently.)

Interviewer: *By the North Gate,* your first book, is a collection of
short stories, and you continue to publish them. Is the short story
your greatest love? Do you hold with the old adage that it is more
difficult to write a good story than a novel?

Oates: Brief subjects require brief statements. There is *nothing* so
difficult as a novel, as anyone knows who has attempted one; a short
story is bliss to write set beside a novel of even ordinary proportions.

But in recent years I haven't been writing much short fiction. I
don't quite know why. All my energies seem to be drawn into longer
works. It's probably the case that my period of greatest productivity is
behind me, and I'm becoming more interested in focussing upon a
single work, usually a novel, and trying to "perfect" it section by
section and page by page.

Interviewer: Nevertheless, you've published more short stories,
perhaps, than any other serious writer in America today. I remember
that when you chose the 21 stories to compose *The Wheel of Love,*
you picked from some ninety which had been in magazines the two
years since your previous collection. What will become of the seventy
or so stories you didn't include in that collection? Were some added
to later collections? Will you ever get back and pick up uncollected
work?

Oates: If I'm serious about a story I preserve it in book form;
otherwise I intend it to be forgotten. This is true of course for poems
and reviews and essays as well. I went back and selected a number of
stories that for thematic reasons were not included in *The Wheel of
Love,* and put them into a collection called *The Seduction and Other
Stories.* Each of the story collections is organized around a central

theme and is meant to be read as a whole—the arrangement of the stories being a rigorous one, not at all haphazard.

Interviewer: You don't drink. Have you tried any consciousness-expanding drugs?

Oates: No. Even tea (because of caffeine) is too strong for me. I must have been born with a rather sensitive constitution.

Interviewer: Earlier you mentioned Hugh Petrie in *The Assassins*. He is but one of many deranged characters in your books. Have you known any genuine madmen?

Oates: Unfortunately, I have been acquainted with a small number of persons who might be considered mentally disturbed. And others, strangers, are sometimes drawn my way; I don't know why.

Last week when I went to the university, I wasn't allowed to teach my large lecture class because, during the night, one of my graduate students had received a telephone call from a very angry, distraught man who announced that he intended to kill me. So I had to spend several hours sequestered away with the head of our department and the head of security at the university and two special investigators from the Windsor City Police. The situation was more embarrassing than disturbing. It's the first time anyone has so explicitly and publicly threatened my life—there have been shy, indirect threats made in the past, which I've known enough not to take seriously.

(The man who called my student is a stranger to us all, not even a resident of Windsor. I have no idea why he's so angry with me. But does a disturbed person really need a reason. . . ?)

Interviewer: How about the less threatening, but nonetheless hurtful, reactions of friends and relatives—any reactions to conscious or unconscious portraits in your work?

Oates: My parents (and I, as a child) appear very briefly in *Wonderland,* glimpsed by the harassed young hero on his way to, or from, Buffalo. Otherwise there are no portraits of family or relatives in my writing. My mother and father both respond (rather touchingly at times), to the setting of my stories and novels, which they recognize. But since there is nothing of a personal nature in the writing, I have not experienced any difficulties along those lines.

Interviewer: Aside from the singular incident at the university, what are the disadvantages of being famous?

Oates: I'm not aware of being famous, especially here in Windsor, where the two major bookstores, Coles', don't even stock my books. The number of people who are 'aware' of me, let alone who read my writing, is very small. Consequently I enjoy a certain degree of invisibility and anonymity at the university, which I might not have at an American university—which is one of the reasons I am so much at home here.

Interviewer: Are you aware of any personal limitations?

Oates: Shyness has prevented me from doing many things; also the amount of work and responsibility here at Windsor.

Interviewer: Do you feel you have any conspicuous or secret flaw as a writer?

Oates: My most conspicuous flaw is . . . well, it's so conspicuous that anyone could discern it. And my secret flaw is happily secret.

Interviewer: What are the advantages of being a woman writer?

Oates: Advantages! Too many to enumerate, probably. Since, being a woman, I can't be taken altogether *seriously* by the sort of male critics who rank writers 1, 2, 3 in the public press, I am free, I suppose to do as I like. I haven't much sense of, or interest in, competition; I can't even grasp what Hemingway and the epigonic Mailer mean by battling it out with the other talent in the ring. A work of art has never, to my knowledge, displaced another work of art. The living are no more in competition with the dead than they are with the living. . . . Being a woman allows me a certain invisibility. Like Ellison's *Invisible Man.* (My long journal, which must be several hundred pages by now, has the title *Invisible Woman.* Because a woman, being so mechanically judged by her appearance, has the advantage of hiding within it—of being absolutely whatever she knows herself to be, in contrast with what others imagine her to be. I feel no connection at all with my physical appearance and have often wondered whether this was a freedom any man—writer or not— might enjoy.)

Interviewer: Do you find it difficult to write from the point of view of the male?

Oates: Absolutely not. I am as sympathetic with any of my male characters as I am with any of my female characters. In many respects I am closest in temperament to certain of my male characters—Nathan Vickery of *Son of the Morning,* for instance—

and feel an absolute kinship with them. "The Kingdom of God *is* within."

Interviewer: Can you tell the sex of a writer from the prose?

Oates: Never.

Interviewer: What male writers have been especially effective, do you think, in their depiction of women?

Oates: Tolstoy, Lawrence, Shakespeare, Flaubert. . . . Very few, really. But then very few women have been effective in their depiction of them.

Interviewer: Do you enjoy writing?

Oates: I do enjoy writing, yes. A great deal. And I feel somewhat at a loss, aimless and foolishly sentimental, and disconnected, when I've finished one work and haven't yet become absorbed in another. All of us who write work out of a conviction that we are participating in some sort of communal activity. Whether my role is writing, or reading and responding, might not be very important. I take seriously Flaubert's statement that we must love one another in our art as the mystics love one another in God. By honoring one another's creation we honor something that deeply connects us all, and goes beyond us.

Of course writing is only one activity out of a vast number of activities that constitute our lives. It seems to be the one that some of us have concentrated on, as if we were fated for it. Since I have a great deal of faith in the process and the wisdom of the unconscious, and have learned from experience to take lightly the judgements of the ego, and its inevitable doubts, I never find myself constrained to answer such questions. Life is energy, and energy is creativity. And even when we as individuals pass on, the energy is retained in the work of art, locked in it and awaiting release if only someone will take the time and the care to unlock it . . .

The Emergence of Joyce Carol Oates

Lucinda Franks/1980

From *The New York Times Magazine*, 27 July 1980, 22, 26, 30, 32, 43-44, 46. © 1980 The New York Times Co. Reprinted by permission.

In a trance Raphael stretched out upon his raft. . . . The pond had made itself manifest to him. It took him into its depth, it embraced him, whispered . . . "Come here, come here to me, I will take you in. I will give you new life."

The undersized child with . . . that furtive expression tinged with a melancholy irony . . . was seen less and less frequently that summer until, finally, one morning, it was discovered that he had simply vanished. . . . "Raphael," they called. . . . "Where are you hiding?" . . . They went in search of him to Mink Pond, of course. . . . But where was Mink Pond? It seemed, oddly, that Mink Pond, too, had vanished.

—From *Bellefleur* by Joyce Carol Oates

She slides back the glass doors, steps out onto her stone terrace and invites you, for a short time, to enter her world. A hawk dips down through the trees, a cat and dog face off with hisses and growls. You recognize all of them: a gallery of misplaced characters. The bird belongs not here in Joyce Carol Oates's backyard on the outskirts of Princeton, N.J., but elsewhere and you half expect it to swoop down and ferry you to Bellefleur Castle; the rainbow-colored cat, the holly, the dragonflies, all are escapees from the author's 35th and latest book.

Beyond the terrace, a familiar body of water, choked with rushes and water iris, stretched languidly before you.

"Yes, it's Mink Pond," says the author. "That, like many things in the land of the Bellefleurs, is a symbol. No! Raphael did not die. The pond is an emblem of his imagination—a more hospitable place for him—and that, in the end, is where he returned."

And, in the end, all the raw pieces of reality—the people, places, bits of gossip, confession—that touch the life of Joyce Carol Oates are, like Raphael, swallowed up in her imagination, transformed, compresed, cut and set like diamonds in her fiction.

The cat, Misty, oblivious of the fact that he has been re-created in his mistress's literature as the dazzling Mahalaleel—an aristocratic stray who as the *grand-chat* of Bellefleur Castle is more iridescent, much silkier and infinitely more commanding than the original—lurks beneath the garden chairs waiting to pounce on one of his brothers, all of whom had been rescued by the author, who is childless, from a roadside abandonment.

She sits casually, but she is as tall and erect as a signal tower, fading in and out each time a blue jay or cat intercepts her attention. She looks somehow lost in time, as though she has emerged from the Gothic porticos of her own *Bellefleur*. If her face is dramatically arresting, she seems to dress it down with the ordinary. At first impression—dainty hairstyle, rosebud lips, Middle Western drawl— she looks as if a frilly apron or wrist flower would suit her. But then, there are the eyes: intense, brown, shining; twice as big and taking in twice as much as you might expect.

She speaks almost below her breath, as though there were someone in the next room who she didn't want to overhear her. It is hard to believe that this is the voice directing the stories that tell of sons who murder their mothers, of religious leaders who gouge out their own eyes, of medical students who cannibalize cadavers.

She reminds you of a magician's sleeve, from which a chain of connected handkerchiefs is pulled; it doesn't seem possible (the sleeve is not very wide), but the material keeps coming and coming until it fills the stage. There are many worlds, you realize, belonging to Joyce Carol Oates, beyond the one which you are being permitted to visit.

Winner of the National Book Award for fiction in 1970 for her novel *them,* frequent recipient of an O. Henry Award, a member of the American Academy and Institute of Arts and Letters, Joyce Carol Oates is regarded as one of the nation's preeminent fiction writers. Nevertheless, at age 42, she has not received the popular recognition accorded her equals, largely because in the past she herself has chosen obscurity, refusing interviews and talk-show invitations. In the last 17 years, she had produced 12 novels, 11 collections of short stories, eight volumes of poetry, three books of literary criticism, one play, and hundreds of book reviews. That is an average of about two books a year, a record of prolificacy that has earned not only the awe but also the suspicion of many critics, who accuse her of "automatic writing." She has always, however, enjoyed a rather rarefied audience, with a group of only about 20,000 faithful buying her books in hard cover.

Now, however, with the publication of *Bellefleur,* hopes abound that this state of affairs will change. Unlike her other books, which are fixed in time and place and usually deal with a specific genre group, *Bellefleur* spans six generations of an American family, beginning with one Jean-Pierre Bellefleur who, having been banished from France, builds in 1802 a castle in the valleys of a place that sounds very much like the Adirondacks. It is a Gothic saga, a tableau of the real and the surreal, rich with magic, whimsy, tragedy and humor and just the right number of unforgettable characters (some of whom turn into animals from time to time) to fit the prescription for a commercial success. The heads of her publishers are alive with fantasies that she will become the book publishing world's next queen-for-a-day, with her hefty backlist turning into coffers of gold. Fawcett Books, the paperback house that has issued all of her novels, has apparently decided this might happen; it has put in a floor bid of $200,000—$50,000 higher than it has ever paid for a Joyce Carol Oates book—for the as yet unscheduled paperback auction of *Bellefleur.*

Their high hopes may be realized. In last Sunday's *New York Times Book Review,* John Gardner said that "whatever its faults, *Bellefleur* is simply brilliant," and he called Miss Oates "one of the great writers of our time."

> *She walked past the front steps, her hair blowing helplessly across her face. . . . Why was everything so raw, so open? It was like walking along the beach, narrowing her eyes slightly against the wind. She felt a certainty, an excitement, that something would happen very shortly, and that her life would begin.*
>
> —From *Do With Me What You Will*

Deep in the leafy, lazy Princeton street, carpenters are banging, sawing, lifting shovelfuls of earth, building a new wing on the home of Miss Oates and her husband, Raymond Smith, a professor of 18th-century literature. The butterflies fluttering about the terrace seem like metaphors for the feeling of expansion, of something taking flight, for the sides of the house are made of glass.

"I'm so glad you did not come when it was raining," Miss Oates says, bringing out tea, water and soda pop at intervals. "It's so gloomy in a glass house on a dark day."

And more exposed, perhaps, than an earlier self ever would have wished. There was a time when she and her husband lived in an apartment so small that she had to write in her bedroom on a card table. The bookstore in the Canadian town where she taught until two years ago—at the University of Windsor—did not even carry her books. To the New York literary community, she seemed one step away from J. D. Salinger in her upcountry isolation. She liked it just fine that way. It gave her the liberty to be what she wanted to be, free of the pressure of spotlights and literary fashions. It protected her from the terror of being paraded about, examined—a bug on a pin beneath hot lights.

A frequent reviewer for *The New York Times Book Review*, she has refused to read reviews of her own work. In the past, she has instructed her agent not to inform her of any public reaction to her work. And she has never let the person dearest to her in the world— her husband—read the body of her work. Although he reads the occasional book review she writes, virtually all of the rest of her work is off-limits because, she says, "it would be like living with a constant condemnation if he didn't like it." He will escort her to a speech or a reading but then will wait out in the hall. "If she makes a mistake," he reasons, "the mistake dies there. If I am present, it lives on."

"He would like to read my work," she says, "but it is not a burning issue between us. There is no pressure on him, or me, and it makes life easier."

Although frail, Miss Oates has an extraordinary physical presence (its impact is as startling as coming upon a deer in the middle of a wood), and the secret of that may rest in her solemnity, her reserve, a kind of power of concealment. So emotion-bound does she become in anything that she is writing that life itself is often too strenuous. She does not smoke or drink, and even tea is too strong for her. Highly sensitive and receptive, she is a kind and generous friend to young writers. Yet there is an aloofness as she appraises people from behind rose-tinted glasses, a guardedness that makes it difficult for anyone to get to know her.

Nevertheless, there is a second Joyce Carol Oates taking form and it is as though she were becoming, in a certain sense, not unlike one of her own characters. She creates people who isolate themselves from the complexity of their worlds, who cast about in states of narcissism and hubris, trying to impose their own single-visioned reality on the chaos of life, or who retreat altogether into cataleptic states of denial. Almost always, these characters find redemption and survival by accepting the natural order of the universe, by resigning themselves to the fact that there is no one answer, no deliverance, by rejoining and flowing with the society around them.

In an external sense, Miss Oates has embarked on a kind of reunion of her own. For the first time, she has expressed an interest in knowing the details of advance sales bids and promotional data on her new novel. Eager to debunk the assumption that she is a recluse writing in "a fever possessed," she brings out the notes and drafts of *Bellefleur,* staggering beneath a pile that contains plot charts, maps and the Bellefleur family trees.

This spring, another precedent was broken. She and her husband went to Western and Eastern Europe, a six-week tour that included attending literary symposiums and giving speeches. It was her first time on a airplane since she left college.

The shift began, friends say, when she accepted a position of visiting professor of creative writing at Princeton University in 1978. Until then, she had clung to a tightly circumscribed life. Born in the five-house town of Millersport, on the shoulders of the Erie Canal, Joyce Carol Oates went to Syracuse University on a scholarship and got her M.A. in English from the University of Wisconsin, where she met and married Smith. She settled down to teach, first at the University of Detroit, then across the river in Ontario at the University of Windsor.

"She grew up in a small place, taught in a small place all her life and now she has undergone a life change," says Evelyn Shrifte, her editor at Vanguard Press, her first publisher. "She has gotten bolder."

This fall will be her third year at Princeton, and there is evidence that she plans to stay permanently. In addition to buying, and even expanding, a house, she and her husband have recently started in their home a small book-publishing press, an off-shoot of *The Ontario Review*, a literary journal which the couple founded in 1974 and which Smith edits.

Even more significant, in December 1978, Joyce Carol Oates changed publishers. Breaking with Vanguard, which had published all of her ficton since her first book in 1963, she signed on with the much larger house of E. P. Dutton, which will promote her books on a much grander scale.

"She has broken a kind of isolation," says her long-time friend and literary agent Blanche Gregory. "She is among professors of great prestige—Princeton was the watering ground of Fitzgerald, you know—and she goes to parties and hops on a train to New York and sees [Donald] Barthelme or John Updike or a dozen others." Miss Oates herself says, "It's a wonderful new experience, being part of a literary community."

She teaches only two writing workshops a week, as opposed to a full course load at Windsor. Whereas the academic world at Windsor was "cold and stark," she says she finds her Princeton students more exciting and exacting.

> *I, too, drift into sleep and am rewarded with astonishing, unspeakable sights. In fact, I have grown to fear sleep, at the very edge of sleep my entire body jerks, waking me. But the visions are not always nightmares. They can be sweet, soothing, hypnotic. I think they are the dreams of others, former occupants of this rented bed. Surely they are not my own.*
>
> —From *Son of the Morning*

Joyce Carol Oates chops shrimp in her pin-neat kitchen, the counters so clear you could somersault the length of them. Humming, she sets the shellfish afloat in a tart and airy yogurt soup. Smith, large, handsome and bashful, emerges from his study. He looks like a man who has lost something. A glance at his wife doing the cooking, and he smiles longingly.

The living room seems oddly untouched: the glass dining table glints with sun; perfectly placed about the room are shiny ashtrays, hanging plants, a collection of old clocks, stacked records. One wonders whether the couple has rearranged both the room and themselves—halted the motion, stopped everything in time—on account of the invasion by this stranger with a note pad. Whatever the reason, they move delicately, as though they were traveling down narrow aisles in a china shop, watched by a crowd of window shoppers with their noses pressed to the glass.

"Some cheese, honey?" she asks, straightening her husband's collar. Smith cuts himself tiny squares of cheese, arranges them on a plate and studies them. He talks—very softly, but as distinctly as if he were addressing a Dictaphone—about putting out *The Ontario Review.* She boasts about how hard he works at it. Their voices drift like a melody above the contrapuntal movements of their hands— hers, reedlike, do a series of arabesques as she lifts spoon to lip; his simply glide about the air—a pas de deux of two spirits that have danced well together for a very long time.

One cannot imagine either of them tearing through the house to catch a train, or throwing an ashtray in exasperation, or even raising their voices.

Instead, they take long bicycle trips, drive about in their car, walk and poke into lost corners of Manhattan. "I also spend an inordinate amount of time," Miss Oates confesses, "doing absolutely nothing."

It is clear, however, that whatever she does, including "nothing," she is a writer who spends sometimes 24 hours a day writing. She once went to bed and dreamed an entire new ending for an already published book, *Wonderland,* which was incorporated in subsequent editions.

"If you are a writer," she says, "you locate yourself behind a wall of silence and no matter what you are doing, driving a car or walking or doing housework, which I love, you can still be writing because you have that space."

Often during the evening, she will curl up on the couch with her pad and pencil and scrawl, like a little girl making up a story. Then, before she goes to bed, she will read over the pages she has written and the notes she has made that day. Where most writers must battle the currents of self-doubt to get to the reverse magnet that is their typewriter, Joyce Carol Oates can hardly resist the pull.

Her study is spare: a large desk with just a few papers scattered about, a file cabinet, a bulletin board tacked with chapter headings, a small settee. "I usually work from about 8:30 A.M. to 1 P.M.; then in the afternoon I'll make telephone calls, or teach, or go to New York.

Then I'll make dinner and then, from about 8 until 11:30, I'll work again."

That adds up to anywhere from one to 10 pages a day, but usually about five, unless she is writing a short story, when she will do a draft in one day. "As I get older, I find I can't write as fast, and I have to rewrite again and again, sometimes as much as 17 times."

Her characters, she says, are composites of real people, but her husband never appears in her books. "He is a loving, tender, kind, wonderful man who does not belong in a novel. People like him are the backbone of the earth, no doubt, but he is not melodramatic or intrusive."

She is currently writing a book about betrayal—the betrayal of the American people by such politicians as Nixon and Kissinger—and about personal disappointment. "I've had friends who have been betrayed by their husbands. It haunts me. That kind of betrayal is the worst. It comes like a sword; to wake up one day and find everything you thought was true is false. You just can't absorb it into your reality.

"If it happened to me, I don't think I could survive it."

> *Gradually she began to see the blood on him. . . . Across the side of his head, shyly turned from her, a stream of blood was moving and soaking into the pillow. . . . She did not move. She could smell his blood. Words came to her again, like an incantation, My brother is to blame, that bastard.*
>
> —From *them*

Whether describing the bloodshed of the slums of Detroit, as she did in *them,* or the clinical butchery inside a hospital, as she did in *Wonderland* (there, a student cuts out a uterus from a cadaver, broils it and eats it), Joyce Carol Oates has been criticized for an excess of exquisitely detailed gore.

She reacts archly to this: "I did not create the streets of Detroit. When I write about a man who murders or commits suicide, where do I get the idea from? From a hundred different sources, from the violence and cynicism that is part of our national character.

"People don't criticize journalists for writing too much about the slaughter in Cambodia. Why should a novelist be singled out for writing about what she sees?"

She often plots her stories from newspaper headlines and she views her writing as a reflection of American life. If Norman Mailer resorts to nonfiction to novelize America (his account of the life of Gary Gilmore in *The Executioner's Song* is called a "truelife novel"), then Joyce Carol Oates only attempts her own reproduction of the nation's larger-than-life characters and events.

"When people say there is too much violence in Oates," she says, "what they are saying is there is too much reality in life."

She does admit, however, that even she finds her material rough to write. "If I have to write a particularly gory part, I distance myself. I forget I am me and enter the scene through the narrator. I simply become a vessel for him."

> *The gallery floor shines, it is so highly polished. . . . You step close to the photographs, you peer anxiously at them. . . . Sunrise, trees, mountains, the remarkable delicacy of light, the blossoming of light in leaves. . . . You want to cry out in amazement that you have not seen anything before; you have never seen the mountains before, though you stare out that bedroom window of yours every day of your life.*
> —From *Childwold*

When Joyce Carol Oates was just 25, she went to New York for the first time. "Oh, her eyes were as wide as an ocean!" says Evelyn Shrifte, her former editor. The young author had come to the big city for the publication by Vanguard of her first book, a short-story collection. "I can see her now. The bells were ringing at St. Pat's and it was magic for her.

"Vanguard had taken a chance on her. She was fresh out of school, and I thought she was a genius," says Miss Shrifte, who still mentions the names of Miss Oates's characters as if they were old friends. "She and Ray stayed at my house. They didn't have much money then and we would sit around at night and I would read and they would read and then, at 11 P.M., we would have Tab and a cookie.

"I am very sad that we lost her and I can't help but think that some of the promotion she's getting is ghastly," Miss Shrifte adds. "We always tried to treat her with dignity. Our ads simply mentioned the name Joyce Carol Oates, as you might mention Beethoven, no explanation needed.

"I never edited her. We didn't care about a best seller, we just cared about her being herself. Well, maybe she *can* be promoted. Maybe that's what she likes now. Maybe it's what she deserves."

Dutton has persuaded Miss Oates to take a royalty rate cut to enable a 558-page book to be retailed at a price accessible to a wider public. The publishing house plans to spend upward of $35,000 on promotion, much more than Vanguard ever spent, and it took the unusual step of distributing 1,000 copies free to booksellers at the American Booksellers Association Convention last June. Most of Miss Oates's previous books have had only etchings or photographs on their covers, but Dutton commissioned an original oil painting for the cover of *Bellefleur.* Trade-journal advertisements proclaim the book as "a breakthrough work . . . the mythic culmination of Joyce Carol Oates's ongoing portrait of American life."

"She's going to get a second kind of reader: ordinary people who might not follow serious literature, but who like a good read," says Karen Braziller, her editor at Dutton. "And what author could be unhappy at selling a few more books?"

> *Month followed month and she failed, she failed to conceive, and it was this word she insisted upon—fail, failed—this word Gideon had to endure.*
> *But now. . . . Now the woman was so wonderfully, so arrogantly pregnant . . . nothing was so real to her now as certain flashes of sensation—tastes, colors, even odors, vague impulses and premonitions—which she interpreted as the baby's continuous dreaming, deep in her body.*
> —From *Bellefleur*

"For years, I had wanted to write *Bellefleur,*" Miss Oates says. "I would collect images along the way—a clavichord I saw, a snatch of conversation I heard—but I never could find the right voice. I would just throw the pages away; I was blocked."

The novel began in her mind with a sudden image of a woman sitting beside a baby in a cradle in a shabby but lushly overgrown walled garden. " 'Oh! I'd love to be there,' I thought. It was a warm, penetrating, nostalgic image," and from there, Oates yearned and dreamed right into the book. She worked intensely from the summer of 1978, when she arrived in Princeton, until the following May, to finish it.

The theme threading through the story of the Bellefleurs is the tragedy of greed, the megalomania in the American character that ultimately leads to self-destruction.

Bellefleur, more than any other Oates novel, took possession of her. "It was very peculiar. It was a puzzle haranguing me. I'd hurry to my desk in the morning and sometimes it would take hours to get going, but I would try to do a chapter a day. I was in a very tense and excited state."

She calls *Bellefleur* her "vampire" novel. "Even talking about it still drains me," she says, looking all at once as though she had left the room. "I've had many such psychic vampire experiences in the past.

"I developed some theories about 19th-century Gothicism while writing the book. Using the werewolf, for instance, is a way of writing about an emotional obsession turning into a kind of animal.

"It seemed a race against time. I guess writers always have this feeling that they will die before they complete their work."

When she finished the last page, a feeling of deep melancholia came over her. "There was nothing to make your heart beat fast, nothing to make you afraid. . . . I felt very homesick, like loving a place you know you will never go back to."

> *How fierce the Hawker Tempest . . . fierce and urgent and combative and never playful, like the other planes. . . . Such an airplane must be freed from the spell of gravity, it must be taken into the air as often as possible. . . .*
>
> *There were so many Bellefleurs, people said, but perhaps most of them had never existed. . . . Though Gideon, of course, certainly existed. At least until the day he committed suicide by diving his airplane into Bellefleur Manor.*
>
> —From *Bellefleur*

When Joyce Carol Oates was a child in Erie County—which has been re-created as the Eden County of many of her books, including *Bellefleur*—she remembers how her father, a tool-and-die designer, loved to fly small airplanes. "It scared my mother and me to death.

"It was a big sport in Millersport. My father loved to get into this little chair with wings; he loved the feel of the wind, like being in a hang glider. It became obsessive with him.

"The youngish men would do stunts, flying low over the house, seeing how close they could get. There were a lot of accidents and I was afraid my father would crash, which he didn't."

But the character Gideon Bellefleur, who also became addicted to the thrill of small planes, did. A lingering childhood fear realized finally in her novel? Thus, perhaps, is the creative mind fueled by a need to unconsciously resolve the wishes and fears of the past.

A harsh note to the children's play. Someone is drunk and angry and someone else is frightened and angry and the others are laughing . . . the others stand about laughing, rude jocular hearty, good-natured, the girl is saying, "Stop, stop! Goddam you, stop!"
—From Childwold

Joyce Carol Oates was a slight, skinny girl. The boys all looked very tall to her. She went to a one-room schoolhouse and then the local junior and senior high schools, and going on the school bus every day was a journey of intimidation and violence.

"It was so rural and everybody intermarried," she says. "There were a lot of mentally retarded kids and the older ones would bully the smaller.

"They were rough and ignorant boys and they quit school usually at 16. They appear in my books now and then. It was exhausting. A continual daily scramble for existence."

As chaos swirled outside, inside the Oates farmhouse it was warm, safe, a watering ground. Her family, Roman Catholic, was multitiered and close-knit. She was attached to her younger brother and sister and the grandparents who lived with them. Her paternal grandfather, who appears often in her work, bought her her first typewriter when she was 14.

"He influenced me greatly," she says, wistful. "I listened to his stories and then I began to pretend to write them; I simulated handwriting before I knew letters. And sometimes I just drew symbols—butterflies, cats, trees."

If there was much that was terrible about where she grew up as a child, there was something attractive about the roughness of that world, the little hamlet, the old graveyard, her friends' ramshackle houses full of children. As she takes her place before the typewriter now, she is drawn again and again back to an earlier self.

"When I remember, I remember sometimes even the time before I was born, when my parents were young," she sighs, looking out through the glass toward her pond. "Childhood is the province of the imagination and when I immerse myself in it, I re-create it as it was, as it could have been, as I wanted—and didn't want—it to be."

Speaking about Short Fiction:
An Interview with Joyce Carol Oates

Sanford Pinsker/1981

From *Studies In Short Fiction*, Summer 1981, 239-43. © 1981 *Studies In Short Fiction*. Reprinted by permission.

Joyce Carol Oates needs no special introduction to readers of contemporary American fiction. Since the publication of *By the North Gate* in 1963, collections of her stories have appeared regularly. She is, as well, a frequent reviewer of other people's short fiction. To both efforts Miss Oates brings unusual amounts of energy and intelligence.

On March 10, 1980, she spent an exhausting day on the Franklin & Marshall campus—visiting classes, answering students' questions (including one that packed a naive, unintentional wallop: "Did your childhood affect you much?") and, of course, reading from her work. Some-where between the end of lunch and the start of a class-room visit, I broached the subject of an interview. I promised not to ask her any autobiographical questions, either about her childhood or about her present situation. She accepted. Then I offered to record our conversation about aspects of the short story and to edit the tape later. This she declined, preferring instead to conduct the con-versation by mail.

So, for the next few months I sent questions and she responded—always promptly and always with the same intensity she had radiated during her visit. Some of my questions did not stimulate, did not inspire. In one postcard she complained of being "overwhelmed with interviews." Nonetheless, she persisted, and the results follow:

Interviewer: I. B. Singer once told me that he thought some subjects were more appropriate to the short story than to longer forms. A dybbuk, for example, could not be the protagonist of a family novel. As far as I know, there are no dybbuks in *your* canon, but would you agree with Singer's general premise—namely, that some subjects are, by definition, appropriate or congenial to the short story?

Oates: I cannot agree that some subjects are by definition appropriate or inappropriate to the short story. The "short story" is a highly elastic term, after all. A brief enigmatic dream-tale by Kafka . . . a dense, meditative, slow-moving story by Henry James . . . a spare exchange of dialogue by Hemingway: all can be considered "stories" yet each differs radically from the others. Surely there is a novelist somewhere who *could* write a family novel with a dybbuk as the protagonist? (In fact I may have done this myself, in a manner of speaking, in my new novel *Bellefleur*).

Interviewer: Not only has criticism of individual short stories or of writers who work principally in this genre been rather sparse, but one gets the feeling that theoretical speculation about short fiction has been almost completely dormant. Am I right about these suspicions? Or put another way: Is there anything new to say about the American short story that Edgar Allan Poe hasn't already said in his famous remarks about Hawthorne's short stories?

Oates: Poe's remarks are inappropriate to our time, and in fact to the marvelous modern tradition of the story that begins with Chekhov, Joyce, Conrad, and James. Speculation about short fiction should probably remain minimal since "speculation" about most works of art is usually a waste of time. Those of us who love the practice of an art often hate theorizing because it is always theorizing based upon past models: as such, it must inevitably incline toward the conservative, the reactionary, the exhortative, the school of *should* and *should not*. Genuine artists create their own modes of art and nothing interests them except the free play of the imagination. Poe's and Hawthorne's impulses in fiction were bound up with the allegorical, the static, and the highly romantic (which is to say, the impersonal). How can one draw a reasonably sober line between Hawthorne, James, Stephen Crane, Faulkner, and Hubert Selby, Jr. . . . ? Where would Beckett or Flannery O'Connor or Saul Bellow fit in? It isn't even true that short stories are necessarily *short*.

Interviewer: One of the continuing myths about you is that you write many of your short stories in a single, long burst of creative energy—often nearly all night—and that in the morning there is a manuscript of yet another Oates story. Is this a fact about how you often work, or, rather, yet another version of the romantic artist that simply isn't true?

Oates: I would be interested in seeing the story or interview that claimed I wrote all night long—since in fact I have never done so. While it is true that my first drafts are almost always written out— often in longhand—in a single long (and draining) burst of what might be called energy, it is always the case that the subsequent drafts are much longer and are often spread out over a period of time. There are always "first drafts" of stories among my worksheets, waiting for their formalization, their re-imagining. What prompts me to begin work on them at a certain time, on a certain day—I can't know. I have never in my life written anything straight out, not even a five-line poem. I have always revised and edited.

Interviewer: Would it be fair to say that you find satirical short stories—especially the ones placed in an academic setting—more congenial than the prospect of a long academic novel? I guess what I mean is this: I can see you writing versions of the stories in *Hungry Ghosts,* but not a book like Mary McCarthy's *Groves of Academe.* (I realize that *Expensive People* has something of this flavor perhaps, but I don't see it primarily as an academic satire.)

Oates: My most recent novel, *Unholy Loves* (1979), is an academic comedy set at an upstate New York university larger than Bennington, smaller than Cornell, prestigious yet not quite competitive with Harvard, Princeton, and Yale.

Interviewer: Some of your stories strike me as thoroughly conventional in technique, some as dazzlingly experimental. Nonetheless, one doesn't normally associate your stories with the work of Barthelme, Sukenick, Sorrentio or others of the Post-Modernist school. Could you comment about the whole matter of "experimentation" with regard to short fiction?

Oates: "Experimentation" for its own sake has never interested me, but if a story's content—if its protagonist—is "post-modernist" in sensibility, then the style of the story will probably reflect this predilection. As time passes and I become more and more comfortable with telling a linear story and populating it with characters, I inevitably become more and more interested in the structures into which fiction can be put, and the kinds of language used to evoke them. But the degree of sophistication of my protagonist usually dictates the degree of sophistication of the story. I admit to a current fascination with the phenomenon of *time*—I seem to want to tell a story as if it were sheer lyric, all its components present simultaneously. The only "stories" that interest me at the present time are long ones—very long. I am fascinated too with the concept of a "novel" shaped out of a sequence of closely related and intertwined "short stories." (My use of quotation marks indicates my skepticism about literary terms.)

Interviewer: Let's pursue your fascination with "sheer lyric" just a bit. I often have the sense that your fiction begins with a powerful, haunting image (e.g. the pack of wild dogs in *Son of the Morning*) that may have surfaced first in a poem (as I *think* was the case with the dogs) or a short story. Do you generally move from shorter units of the imagination to longer ones, or do other considerations bring an image into its proper structure? In this regard, do you work like a painter, going through a series of "studies" in a subject until you find the one that fulfills the image's potential?

Oates: This is very difficult to answer. I think yes, yes I do begin with an image; then again I think—well, no, I obviously begin with an "idea" (the "idea" of trying to create in words a "religious consciousness" set in a recognizable United States, in the era of Born-Again politicians and other hazards to one's mental health . . .) The haunting image of the walled garden in *Bellefleur* was one point of departure for that novel; then again, the hope to create a microcosm of America—imperialist, exploitative, yet tirelessly optimistic—was certainly another. I suppose in some queer way the two evolve together: the image, the idea: and create somehow an adequate structure which can do justice to them both.

Interviewer: Perhaps we can move our discussion of the creative process from the writing desk to the lectern. A good many people who teach poetry workshops grumble that their students are unacquainted with poetry generally, that they don't *read* enough. Indeed, that complaint might also be leveled at those who have more manuscripts of their own to submit than they do individual volumes of poetry on their bookshelves. Do short story writers face similar problems in the classroom? And if so, do they matter as much? At all?

Oates: Prose fiction is probably more generally, because more easily, read. In any case I require an anthology of short stories in my workshops, and we spent a fair amount of time analyzing and discussing other writers. This is not only enormously rewarding in itself—my Princeton students are avid readers, and quite enthusiastic—but, as one might imagine, instructive for all.

Interviewer: We are told constantly that Formalism's heyday is over, that critics have moved beyond the close-reading of texts to larger, more theoretical speculations (Structuralism, Post-Structuralism and the like). At the same time, though, there is still a decided preference for the "teachable" short story when one makes choices for a syllabus in, say, an Introduction to Fiction class. From your point of view, what ought teachers to do? (I realize that this is broadly put, but what I'm angling for is nothing less than this—Are there any advices you might care to give?)

Oates: Teachers follow their instincts—their likes and dislikes—like everyone else. I can't imagine prescribing for anyone else.

Interviewer: I'm sure you've heard the assorted dissatisfactions people have with anthologies, but I wonder if you might comment on one in particular—namely, that anthologies encourage the sad reality of a writer becoming known—and thus labeled—by two or three stories some editor has chosen. Does that fact of publishing life bother you? Would you prefer an anthology—of the sort that sometimes happen in collections of poetry—where the writers, rather than an editor, pick up their respective favorites?

Oates: This is certainly an excellent idea; I know we would all welcome it. But, to my knowledge, it hasn't been done—or at least I have not been involved. (Perhaps you know someone who would enjoy editing such a book.)

Interviewer: Because your short stories appear in such a wide range of magazines and journals, could you give us some indication of how many short stories you have circulating to editors at any given moment? And I'm sure that readers, especially those who are struggling, beginning writers, would be interested in knowing if the pains of rejection slips ever go away completely. Robert Lowell once said something to the effect that when he began writing poetry, it seemed as if he could not get *any* of his poems published. Later, however, he discovered an even greater, more vexing problem when he could get *all* of them accepted. Has that, roughly, been your situation? And if not, why do you think that that's the case?

Oates: Strange as it might sound, I have been writing very few short stories in recent years. All my energies are going into long—very long—works. A "short story" will appear in *Kenyon Review* sometime soon—but it is more than 60 pages long. The novel exerts a powerful fascination for me at the present time—large, ambitious, audacious, playful, "allegorical" structures—which have space enough for variations upon themes, counterpoint, parody, contrasts, historical and social and economic peculiarities, etc.! So I have barely a handful of stories, and perhaps the same number of poems. (In any case, the vagaries of acceptances and rejections are blessedly peripheral to me—dealt with entirely by my agent.)

Interviewer: To conclude, can we go back to some matters of technique you touched on earlier? Am I right in thinking that presenting all the components of a story simultaneously is something of what you are doing in *Childwold?* And if so, could you talk a bit about the technical differences between that book, that texture of writing, and your earliest stories about Eden County. By that I mean, similarities of people and place still persist, but the effect has altered radically. This, I take it, is a function of style, but what else? And too: Do you think that the phenomenon of time is a narrative problem exclusively, or a matter of a protagonist's apprehension of psychological reality, or both?

Oates: Well—the components of a story, unlike those, say, of a painting, cannot be presented simultaneously. And though *Childwold* is frequently image-centered, it quite clearly unfolds in time, and tells a coherent story: indeed, it is meant to point beyond its narrative conclusion, to a "future" beyond the closing paragraph. (That is, Laney's "future" as an independent and even educated young woman—free of Kasch's imagination.) *Bellefleur* is more obviously a "classical," even clockwork, sort of structure, in which the narrative voice (i.e. the author) is serenely experimental, within my own terms of reference.

An Interview with Joyce Carol Oates

Leif Sjoberg/1982

From *Contemporary Literature*, Summer 1982, 269-89. ©
1982 University of Wisconsin Press. Reprinted by permission.

This interview, which originally appeared in the Stockholm
magazine, *Artes,* began at Princeton, where Joyce Carol
Oates is a professor in the Writing division of the English
Department. It was conducted over a period of several
weeks in 1980, and continued through letters and telephone conversations.

Q. Among all the poetry readings at the 92nd Street "Y" that I have
attended, yours was the only one in which the writer held the manuscript up to the audience so that they could see its length. You
wanted to "give warning," as you said, and to prepare your listeners
"for the length of the poem" and the need for "concentration" for
the duration of the poem. It was as if you established an agreement
with your listeners about this particular poem, and when it was read
we all relaxed, and you talked a little about it, quite informally. Have
you done this at other readings, too?

A. I make it a practice to suggest to the audience the relative length
of a poem. This *is* important, but we take it for granted when we read
the printed page, since we absorb the length unconsciously. Of
course, my audience at the "Y" was too large for the necessary sort
of intimacy. At smaller gatherings, or when meeting with university
students, I make certain that they can see the size of the poem, so to
speak.

Q. In one piece that you read, "Leave-taking," there seemed to be
a strong personal element. What was your central purpose in that
poem?

A. I had wanted to give voice to the uncanny, and rather beautiful,
"presence of absence" we sometimes experience when we see the
familiar world emptied of ourselves. So many people have commented on this poem in which the house, emptied of furniture,

101

belongings, and its tenants, has a future and a past, but no present! I was very pleased with the number of personal responses from listeners.

Q. Did I miss something you said in that context about existential matters: doubting one's existence at certain moments, or the like?

A. We *believe* we exist in terms of other people, our surroundings, our activities, or our environment. If these are altered or denied us—what then? Is there a personality that is, to quote Dickinson, a "zero at the bone?" Or is personality nearly all cultural—external trappings? These are questions some of my poems address themselves to.

Q. At this same reading, you mentioned that you had extracted a large portion of a one-thousand page novel manuscript and made prose poems of it. How can that be done without getting the genres all mixed up?

A. My new long novel is a series of interlocking tales, many of them mountain legends, fairy tales, and fabricated history. A typical mountain legend would lend itself easily to the narrative poem structure. The novel itself consists, in part, of prose poem sections. I chose deliberately to bring together the lyric, the epic, and the dramatic in a single experimental form.

A. What do you want to achieve with your poetry?

A. I hope to achieve with my poetry whatever I hope to achieve with my fiction.

Q. And that is?

A. It is a kind of homage or worship, very difficult to explain.

Q. Is inventiveness enough in poetry/art? How important is the corollary, observation, or "discovery," as Stevens put it?

A. I am not a didactic person and cannot feel comfortable prescribing any general rules for poetry. I tend to feel that the practice of poetry is all—the theorizing is often a feeble attempt to justify the practice. I think that, if Stevens could have written as powerfully as Whitman, along Whitman's lines, no doubt he would have. But he could not—so his aesthetic theories differ. The same is true for Eliot, who often teaches cultural prejudices in the guise of poetry.

Remember that poetry is a great, great art—an enormous art—it can accomodate a great multitude of individuals!

Q. O. K. Let's hear what you think of some of them. "The time for Beauty is over," said Pound, and continued, "Mankind may return to it but it has no use for it at present. The more Art develops the more scientific it will be, just as science will become artistic." Do you think we are likely to get more poems closer to science and the methods it employs?

A. I believe that the science most humanists reject is bad science, devoid of human subtlety and imagination. Though I have not the training to appreciate it, I feel fairly certain that higher mathematics and physics can be as beautiful as poetry. Perhaps the inevitable tragedy of our complex civilization is that we must be specialists in our fields—and our fields have become increasingly difficult, so that communication is nearly impossible.

Q. To return to Pound: he must have been of two minds in his views on "learned" poetry, on the one hand, and pure emotional poetry, on the other, since in "A Retrospect" he suggests that "Only emotion endures," and feels it is better to recall those particularly beautiful lines that ring in a person's head rather than locating them and accounting for their source and meaning, as scholars tend to do. What are some of the lines of poetry that have been especially haunting, meaningful, or beautiful to you?

A. Many lines of poetry!—many indeed. Lines from Whitman, Yeats, Frost, Lawrence, Stevens ("Sunday Morning"), Eliot (*Four Quartets* above all), Keats . . . and, of course, Shakespeare, Donne, Wordsworth, Chaucer. For brevity, there is not one quite so uncanny as Emily Dickinson:

> After great pain, a formal feeling comes—
> The Nerves sit ceremonious, like Tombs—
> The stiff Heart questions was it He, that bore,
> And Yesterday, or Centuries before?
>
>   . . .
>
> This is the Hour of Lead—
> Remembered, if outlived,
> As Freezing persons, recollect the Snow—
> First—Chill—then Stupor—then the letting go—

Q. What about Pound?

A. I am quite ambivalent about Pound. Much of his poetry, it seems to me, is shrill and indefensible—as poetry and as wisdom.

Q. I sense that you are not too keen on influences?

A. As a student and teacher of English and American literature I have read literally thousands of poems, by both the classic poets and relatively unknown poets. No doubt there have been innumerable influences, but they are diffuse.

Most American poets have been influenced by Walt Whitman, our most "American" poet, and, to a lesser extent, Emily Dickinson. But I think Dickinson is so unique a voice that it is almost impossible to be influenced by her. Many of us writing now have been influenced—perhaps far in the past—by William Carlos Williams, who is, of course, related to Whitman, too.

Q. I recall a poem you dedicated to the short story writer Flannery O'Connor; is there a connection there?

A. My dedication in that instance indicates a thematic concern rather than any indebtedness to her writing. I was interested in O'Connor's apocalyptic imagination and what I take to be an excessive puritanism in her—a punitive inclination which I do not share.

Q. Do you have a convenient definition of poetry?

A. Poetry is a rite involving language—at its very highest a sacred rite in that it transcends the personality of the poet and communicates its vision, whether explicitly or by indirection, to others. Many poets speak of the almost impersonal nature of their art when it is most pure and inspired.

Q. I would like to ask what poem satisfies you the most among your own works?

A. Always the most recent work; that is, a long poem in *The Atlantic* called "The Present Tense."

Q. If I am not mistaken, you have published nine major novels, ten collections of short stories, five collections of poetry, two books of essays, plays, and anthologies, and at present you are at work on a major novel while teaching. Creativity seems to be your proper element, but the rest of us do not create a great deal, or at least not much of permanent value. Do you feel that you are unusually prolific?

A. I believe I have a reputation for writing a great deal only because the older, healthy tradition of the writer as an extremely hard-working and persistent craftsman is no longer fashionable. It appears that I am somewhat unusual, but measured against Balzac, Dickens, Henry James, Edith Wharton, Dostoevski, and many others, among the serious writers, I am certainly not unusual. I find solace in their example and would place myself—I hope not immodestly, but one must have ideals—in their tradition.

Q. Do you write everyday?

A. Yes, usually for many hours. I write and write and write, and rewrite, and even if I retain only a single page from a full day's work, it is a single page, and these pages add up. As a result I have acquired the reputation over the years of being prolific when in fact I am measured against people who simply don't work as hard or as long.

Q. Do you find this unfair?

A. That goes without saying, but I have learned to be amused rather than hurt or antagonized by certain charges. I take with absolute seriousness Flaubert's claim that "we must love one another in our art as the mystics love one another in God"—and so my dedication to literature springs from a conviction that it is a "mystical" affirmation or our common human bond.

Writing and, of course, reading are quite simply, for me, the most transcendent of experiences. Even ostensibly violent or despairing literature, like Beckett's, for instance, or much of Faulkner's, I interpret in James Joyce's words as underscoring the eternal affirmation of the human spirit. I am somewhat embarrassed to be speaking in such terms, but those are my beliefs. That I am so passionately committed is probably evidenced by my presumed proliferousness! But even so mandarin a writer as Nabokov—whom I admire, but with qualifications—manages to be prolific, when his total oeuvre is examined.

Q. Coming back to the question of your own creativity. Is there a compulsive element in all this activity . . . ?

A. I assure you, there is very little that is compulsive about my life, either in my writing or otherwise. I believe that the creative impulse is natural in all human beings, and that it is particularly powerful in children unless it is suppressed. Consequently, one is behaving normally and instinctively and healthily when one is creating—literature, art, music, or whatever. An excellent cook is also creative! I am disturbed that a natural human inclination should, by some Freudian turn of phrase, be considered compulsive—perhaps even pathological. To me this is a complete misreading of the human enterprise. One should also enjoy one's work, and look forward to it daily.

Surprisingly enough, over the years I have come to be more and more certain of these beliefs. I am possibly more dedicated to teaching now than I was in my early twenties, and the same is true about my feelings toward literature. In the past twenty years I have seen my ideals affirmed rather than eroded. Of course I have difficult days with my writing, but in general all that I have just said is true for every hour of my life.

Q. Swedish literature is, of course, far from lacking in violence, but it has tended to emphasize sex rather than violence, while American literature—and TV—tend to be more violent. What is your rationale for employing the theme of violence so often in your books?

A. I don't accept charges that I am unduly violent in my writing. Most of my novels and stories are explorations of the contemporary world interpreted in a realist mode, from what might be called a tragic and humanistic viewpoint. Tragedy always upholds the human spirit because it is an exploration of human nature in terms of its strengths. One simply cannot know strengths unless suffering, misfortune, and violence are explored quite frankly by the writer.

Q. In the case of Balzac, who was so enormously productive, there was a plan, which, as you know, later became *La Comédie humaine.* Since your books all seem to deal with American social unrest, are you following a specific plan in your own writing?

A. I certainly do have a general plan for my writing. But I am not accustomed to making statements about my writing, since this seems like self-advertisement. I would prefer to allow the books to stand on their own—even at the risk of being misinterpreted from time to time. Though I am ambitious about my writing I am not ambitious about my career in terms of recognition. Some understanding and sympathetic readers are the most I dare hope for.

Q. You can't leave the questions half answered like that . . .

A. Since approximately 1965 I have set myself the task, in both novels and short stories, of exploring contemporary society on many levels. My focus has been a close examination of the sources of power. The political and economic milieu; professions like medicine, the law, and most recently education and religion; and, to some extent, the predicament of the young and of women—all these have fascinated me.

Q. What is your position on women's liberation?

A. I am very sympathetic with most of the aims of feminism, but cannot write feminist literature because it is too narrow, too limited. I am equally sympathetic with male characters as with female, which has been a source of irritation to some feminist critics. . . . An unfortunate situation, but one which I cannot help.

Q. In his book *The Progress of the Human Mind* Condorcet gives an outline of history that ends on a hopeful note: that equality of men, equality of nations, and also "the real improvement of men" would some day come about. Since 1794 when his essay appeared, we have seen small wars, large wars, world wars, despotism, totalitarianism, natural disasters, the Holocaust, failures of all kinds. How do you assess the chances for "improvement" of the human condition?

A. First I must state my position about all forms of creativity, including my own: these acts are gratuitous offerings and bring something—a vision, an argument, an illumination of a certain corner of the world, a style, a music, an aspect of personality—into the world which did not previously exist. The creative act is an *acute gratuite*. It withdraws nothing from the world—not the intellectual world, not the material world. At its base it is a spontaneous birth, usually presented to the world as an offering or gift. Consequently the creative act and its product are an end in themselves, complete. Like a bird's song—on a much higher structural level. The artist is forever being called upon in the United States to justify himself or herself: and in a way that for instance the manufacturer of toothpaste, automobiles, cigarettes, every sort of material goods is not.

My feeling about art in every form is that, first, it is primarily a natural, spontaneous, inevitable motion of the soul, unique in our species; and, second, that it becomes transformed as it is directed toward a certain social, moral or religious context—at which point it generally acquires its "moral" dimension.

I am responding, of course, to your questions *only* in the spirit of the second category. My persistent and fundamental belief is that art is an expression of the human soul and need not ever, in any circumstances, justify its existence.

Q. And the "human condition" . . .

A. It has been greatly—enormously—in fact miraculously improved. One simply cannot look at the civilized world as it exists

today, in 1980, and compare it to an abstract Platonic condition of
perfection. Improvement exists in nearly every sphere of life, particularly domestic and social life, in civilized nations of the West, and
elsewhere. One must go slowly, of course, and prudently, always with
an awareness that Utopia is a myth, but if one considers the
conditions of workers, for instance, in both the United States and
Europe—not simply wages and work-hours, but working conditions,
benefits, pensions—the progress within a few decades has been
astonishing. I speak as the child of a working class family.

Q. Where did your family come from?

A. My maternal grandparents emigrated from Budapest in the
early years of the twentieth century. Working and living conditions
were extremely difficult at that time, as one might imagine.

In another sphere, that of women's rights, immense progress has
been made. It is simply too easy to cast one's eye about to find faults,
set-backs, "imperfections." They will always exist, our world is not
Utopia. I could speak at great length on this subject, because I feel
strongly about it.

Q. How do you relate to the "past?"

A. There is nothing more absurd than to hear someone, often an
intellectual, speak romantically of the past: the nineteenth century, in
which children of eight or nine toiled in sweat-shops; the medieval
period, in which mad religious struggles killed so many people; even
antiquity, when the Greeks, a refined people, held onto their slaves
and denied citizenship to women! Only someone without a realistic
historical perspective can believe sincerely that "the past" is superior
to the present.

Q. What do you think the arts can do to improve or develop
people?

A. It was said by W. B. Yeats that "tragedy breaks down the dykes
between people." This is true, and it is true for comedy as well. As
soon as one opens a book, by an American, a Japanese, a South
African, a Hungarian, one is in the consciousness of another. The
psychological and emotional act of reading has yet to be fully
explored or understood. In no other art is this really possible. For
instance, I have taught classes of as many as 130 students, working
with them on novels like Mishima's *Confession of a Mask*, which in
many ways is a difficult novel for North American students to
understand. Within a few days the students' sympathy and interest

are remarkable. Or consider the work of Anzia Yezierska, a Jewish writer of the 1920s and 30s, now little known, whose novels about immigrant life on the Lower East Side did so much to bridge the gap between her people and Americans. Abraham Lincoln, meeting Harriet Beecher Stowe, commented that *here* was the person who had brought about the Civil War, hence the freeing of the slaves.

Q. Auden used to say that none of his poems had saved the life of a single Jew during the Hitler era . . .

A. That may be, but in recent times one might think of Solzhenitsyn. One can hardly measure the effect his books have had upon the world, politically as well as emotionally. It would be possible for me to name many writers who have had a considerable impact upon their culture, in both private and public ways. Dickens, for instance, Dostoevski. And Yeats, whose effect upon Irish nationalists was great.

Q. What can your own books do in that direction? Or, what would you want them to do?

A. Evidently my books are taught in university classes in various parts of the world. I can't be certain, however, *how* they are taught . . . or even how accurately they are translated. At a recent conference of Soviet and U.S. writers it was explained to me that my books were read in the Soviet Union, apparently with sympathy. I am surprised to learn that a group of short stories sold quite well in Hungary.

But, of course, I would be very modest about claiming that my books might "improve" humanity. The writer hopes to reach out to a reader . . . to a single reader at a time. The proper object of the writer's hope is not a crowd but an individual. Beyond that it is vainglorious to speculate. Writers who might be accused of being extremely self-absorbed, like Flaubert, for example, often create works of art that are devastating in their power to arouse sympathy in others.

Q. Take someone like Joyce . . .

A. Yes, it is rarely commented upon that his *Ulysses* is a masterpiece of empathy, for Leopold Bloom, the lonely Jew, who is at once a Dubliner and a member of the human species: an extraordinary creation for a writer whose reputation is generally considered elitist.

Q. Are your books used in courses in departments other than the English department?

A. At least in the United States; in sociology, for instance, or psychology, and then I am a bit apprehensive. For though the writer naturally hopes that various kinds of insights and information might be gleaned from his/her work, she/he does create a work of art primarily, which must obey its own internal laws of structure and aesthetic resonance. But I never write to lure the reader, or to "entertain," in the light sense of the word.

Q. Why not?

A. There are quite enough entertainments, especially in America, at the present time.

Q. But to diminish, mitigate or lessen problems?

A. Never! And never to solve problems by authorial fiat. My personal experience—both as a reader and a teacher of literature—is that difficult and troubling works of art, *King Lear*, for instance, are far more beneficial than happy works. One learns so much from Thomas Mann, Dostoevski, Kafka, Melville, and other great writers precisely because they refused to soften their vision of humanity. Yet, even including Kafka, they are by no means negative. I have written an essay on Kafka's mysticism, in particular his relationship to Taoism. He is a much misunderstood writer!

Q. Like many of his contemporaries, Condorcet hoped that science would explain human behavior. What hopes do you have for science in this respect?

A. Once again, outlawing the very concept of Utopia or perfection, I must say that science and its subsequent technology has done immeasurable good for mankind. Science is, of course, of two kinds, theoretic and practical. In the first category we might very well place great philosophical thinkers, for instance, who have helped mankind think its way through superstitions and other forms of ignorance. Great scientists, like Einstein, are usually mystics, guided by impulses (perhaps laws?) of creativity they cannot understand. I am convinced that the great scientists, like the great artists, are expressions of the evolutionary motion of a species.

Q. What would you say the novel has done which science has failed to do?

A. The novel, like all forms of art, is an expression of a subjectivity which might then be translated into the *universal,* while science deals only with the universal or the representative. One of the little-understood responsibilities of the artist is to bear witness—in almost a

religious sense—to certain things. The experience of the concentration camps . . . the experience of suffering, the humiliation of
any form of persecution. Ralph Ellison's novel *Invisible Man* is a
brilliant portrayal of the experience of one black man in America—
one cannot read it without being deeply moved . . . . The experience
of being a woman in a patriarchal culture . . . . Any form of
subjectivity that resonates with universal power complements the
function of science, the objective discipline.

Q. The gap seems to be widening between serious literature and
light literature. Serious, intellectual literature requires more and more
commentaries, it appears, for fewer and fewer readers. Is there, in
your opinion, a risk that literature is becoming too intellectual?

A. No. I cannot agree that the gap is widening between serious
literature and light literature! Our great age of modernism, in English,
at least, is past. Though we read Joyce and, to a lesser extent, Pound,
though we admire Henry James immensely, most of us who are
serious about our writing have no interest in the high modernist
position. One can point confidently to a writer of genius who has
never been a self-consciously coy artist, and who has written books—
at least one of them a masterpiece—that can be read by nearly
anyone: Saul Bellow.

Q. What other writers are readily accessible?

A. Bernard Malamud. John Updike. Iris Murdoch. John Fowles,
and many others.

Q. What about poetry?

A. We are, perhaps temporarily, in a period in American poetry in
which difficulty, obscurantism, and private allusions are applauded by
the critics, sometimes with justification—for a highly self-conscious
writer, like Yeats himself, can also be an extraordinarily good writer.
Certainly there are extremely obscure experimental writers—but their
influence on the culture is quite minimal. Some of them are friends of
mine—and so I can appreciate the sincerity of their art. It is their art;
they haven't much choice about its degree of difficulty. Since I prefer
Saul Bellow's writing to that of his experimental contemporaries, and
since his books have been translated widely, and have made an
impact, I can't feel pessimistic about this problem. Garcia Marquez's
One Hundred Years of Solitude is another recent phenomenon: a
lengthy, difficult, rather quirky novel in Spanish that has sold more

than *Don Quixote!* Offhand I would say that in the U. S. the gap was far more serious in the nineteenth century. One can scarcely believe how our American masterpieces were ignored in favor of utterly insipid, improbable "novels" which became fantastic best sellers and are now completely forgotten. For a serious American writer—especially for a woman writer—this is by far the best era in which to live.

Q. How would you define your concept of beauty? And why is there so much sordidness in your books?

A. Beauty is a cultural ideal, often a cultural prejudice. In the abstract it really cannot exist, for even Einsteinian standards of "Spinozan calm" have meaning only within the human imagination.

In my more recent stories there is probably less that is disturbing or violent since I have become far more concerned with the tragic within the human spirit. In *Son of the Morning,* the most extreme violence is that which occurs when the divine and the human intersect—and this is a subjective, interior experience, difficult to explain in ordinary language.

It should perhaps be re-emphasized that literature—particularly dramatic literature—focuses upon the moment in lives at which conflicts erupt. Think of Ibsen, Strindberg, Chekhov, and of course Shakespeare! Consequently it seems to concern itself with conflict; but this is not, strictly speaking, true. It concerns itself with the momentum of lives, the accumulating fears, tensions, lies, and illusions that then erupt on stage within a two- or three-hour duration. So very economic and condensed an art always appears to be more violent, or sordid, than in fact it is.

Q. Obviously it would be boring if there were too much sameness, if we were all alike, like polished grains of rice. The unusual, the unpredictable, that which is different, should command our interest. But why are so many of your most important characters on the boundaries of sanity?

A. Sanity, too, is a cultural prejudice, especially in nations that insist upon conformity in public affairs, like the United States. Many of the most imaginative and original thinkers—from Mozart to Newton to Einstein to Emily Dickinson—can be too casually dismissed by "normal" people as eccentrics. I agree with recent criticism of the psychiatric profession that focuses upon narrow and outmoded standards of normality and sanity against which people are presumably measured. Can Oedipus, King Lear, Ivan Karamazov, and Faulkner's doomed heroes be casually categorized as mad? On the contrary, it has always seemed to me, even as a much younger woman—as a high school student, in fact—that insane behavior of many kinds was the norm in our society.

Q. Would you give an example of what you have in mind?

A. As children of eleven and twelve we were forced to participate in "atomic bomb" drills and told "Better dead than red!"—the idea being that the United States and Soviet Russia might blow up the world within a few years, and that this probably would have to happen since neither could tolerate the other's existence. Other aspects of collective madness, many of them frankly absurd, impressed upon me the fact that the individual who thinks for himself or herself, critically and unsentimentally, would probably be branded as eccentric or even crazy in such a society. I do not exactly accept the statement that many of my most important characters are on the boundaries of sanity: it seems to me that these people extend the boundaries—that they are not to be measured by the usual conformist standards.

Q. In the event critics would venture to state that you tend to repeat yourself, how would you reply?

A. I am not really aware of repetition within my work. Each novel is a stylistic and structural experiment, from my point of view. Of course, all writers repeat themes, one way or another . . . Proust, Joyce, Faulkner, Bellow, certainly Kafka, Beckett, and others—but it is to be hoped that a new angle of vision, or a newer depth, makes the work innovative. Since I have written more than 300 short stories, for instance, it is perhaps unavoidable that some themes might be repeated; but from my personal point of view each project is new, and addresses itself to new problems and explorations. I am currently much interested in the drama, for instance, which forces a new perspective, and is very stimulating indeed.

Q. Do you think you have learned more from books or people? I refer particularly to books by others, but perhaps also to your own books, or writing them.

A. But one cannot distinguish between books and people! An excellent study of Mozart, for instance, leads us deeply into Mozart; a novel by Faulkner leads us into an aspect of human nature we have perhaps not yet encountered; poetry by one's friends and close colleagues reveals an angle of vision, and often a depth, or soul, not available in ordinary social discourse. No novelist scorns or under-values reality, of course, for this is the very life-blood of our art: close observation of people, places, customs, beliefs, practices.

The writer also learns immensely from his own writing—for each work of art, particularly the lengthy ones, demands an immersion in thinking and experience that would not ordinarily be one's own; and of course the discipline in creating such long works is very strict and very rewarding. D. H. Lawrence believed that the novel was, among other things, an arena for the testing of the author's ideas—those which were weak would be revealed as weak, and those which were strong would triumph. This is perhaps not always the case, for there are powerful works of art whose "ideas" sometimes seem question-able but which satisfy as aesthetic accomplishment none the less.

Q. Whom did you have in mind?

A. Beckett, whose extreme nihilism puzzles me . . .

Q. This may be a ticklish question, but how do you rate some of your contemporaries?

A. I would not rate them, since it is offensive to my principles to "rate" human beings, especially in such very subjective terms.

But Faulkner is clearly the most significant writer. Hemingway is second. Others should not be rated along the same scale at all; they cannot be spoken of in the same context as Faulkner and Hemingway. I can't evaluate Dreiser and Sinclair Lewis, for example, as "artists," only as writers who have contributed important commentaries on social life in America. Dreiser's curious elephantine "mysticism"—in *Sister Carrie*, for example, when he speaks of an inevitable evolution, a "progress" in history—is intellectually indefen-sible. Lewis, though a good satirist, lacks subtlety and a sense of the depth of human experience.

Q. Among the older American authors Eudora Welty and Katherine Anne Porter are supposed to belong to your favorites?

A. Eudora Welty is a favorite of nearly everyone! A very fine, wise writer, less ambitious than the other authors we just mentioned, of course; but within the range of her intention she is completely successful. Of non-American women writers Isak Dinesen is much-admired.

Q. What are your standards in determining what is important in literature?

A. Standards of greatness must encompass depth of vision; a breadth of actual work; a concern for various levels of human society; a sympathy with many different kinds of people; an awareness of and concern with history, or at least contemporary history; a sense of the interlocking forces of politics, religion, economics, and the mores of the society; concern with aesthetics; perhaps even experimentation in forms and language; and above all a "visionary" sense—the writer is not simply writing for his own sake, but to speak to others as force-fully as possible.

Q. It seems obvious especially in your later works that Jung is of importance to you. What books of his have you read and what have you got out of them?

A. I am a voracious reader, and Jung is one of innumerable writers and thinkers I have read. Since I cannot accept his theories on the "male" and "female" archetypes I am not a "Jungian"—but I find his exploration of the Unconscious extremely intriguing. He is quite dif-ferent from Freud, who imagines the unconscious as an adversary to consciousness. Jung understands that the wellsprings of life—creativity above all—reside in the Unconscious and its functions.

In Jung one confronts a bold, original, and "poetic" imagination, valuable for the questions it raises as much as for the answers it hopes to provide. I would set Jung beside Nietzsche; both men are brilliant, and brilliantly provocative. One need not *believe* in their theories in order to learn from them.

Q. To what extent do you study influences with your writing students?

A. It is dangerous to place too much emphasis upon influences; this is a critical method of the past decade, as you know, exemplified by the Yale critic Harold Bloom, which has recently been subjected to wide and quite convincing rejection. Most novelists and poets are probably most powerfully influenced by their early surroundings: they wish to capture universal truths in the form of particular, even local types, and give life to the larger element of the human psyche by way of familiar images.

Q. You have indicated that it is the restless who interest you as a novelist, "for only out of restlessness can higher personalities emerge, just as, in a social context, it is only out of occasional surprises and upheavals that new ways of life can emerge." In what way can we expect that this point of view will be employed in your future novels?

A. My next novel, which is my most ambitious and also longest to date, is a complex parable of American aspirations and tragic shortcomings.

Q. Have you already decided on a title?

A. It is called *Bellefleur* and is imagined in the symbolist mode, though its concerns are very historical. It covers a period of time from approximately the American War of Independence until the present day, though time is treated symbolically. The elder members of the powerful Bellefleur family are destroyed but, one by one, their children—who may represent a younger or at any rate more selfless and idealistic America—escape their influence, and achieve their independence apart from the family's authority.

Q. That sounds like both tragedy and comedy.

A. It is. It is a tragedy in that many people are destroyed, in both a spiritual and literal sense, and a comedy in the higher sense that the instinct for survival and self-determination is celebrated. It was a considerable challenge for me, as the author, to imagine a conclusion that was both tragic and comic simultaneously . . . *Bellefleur* is, as I said, quite long, and filled with many characters and stories, all of them centering upon the American dream in both its daylight and nightmare aspects.

Q. Isn't there a certain risk that a work that mixes tragedy and comedy will be misinterpreted?

A. Sure. It has happened before. One of my longest books, *The Assassins,* was misunderstood by more than one critic. But if the new book is viewed as a poetic analysis of America, its meanings should not be elusive.

Q. Some of your short stories, such as "The Lady with the Pet Dog" and "Metamorphosis," are related to the work of familiar writers. Is this technique a lower form of creativity, not entirely original?

A. Postmodern writing often gains a secondary meaning by its juxtaposition to other works of literature or art. The stories stand on their own and were, of course, published on their own, but they are meant to have an allusive quality. Contrast is, of course, gained—but also a curious and ironic sympathy. The great writers were once young and unknown and struggling merely to be published; their works were not pronounced "great" for many years. I think the similarities between us all are far stronger than one might commonly realize.

Q. What are your feelings about experimentation? I would assume that a master stops experimenting at a certain point.

A. All serious writers are interested in experimentation. It is a means by which they honor their craft.

Q. Are there critical assumptions from which your stories operate?

A. The short story is the form in which I have worked most with experimentation. Virtually each story is an attempt to do something different—consequently it is extremely difficult for me to speak of my short stories in general terms. They proceed from a basis of psychological realism; however, often they take place in an individual's mind. I have become more and more interested in recent years in developing stories that are really miniature novellas: stories that deal with a person's entire life, greatly condensed and focused. An example would be "Daisy" in the 1978 volume *Night-Side*, which deals in a surrealist manner with some of the issues involved in the relationship between sanity and insanity—the story is based very informally on James Joyce's relationship with his schizophrenic daughter Lucia. Another story from the same volume, "A Theory of Knowledge," is a poetic attempt to dramatize the contradictions inherent in philosophizing—in abstracting from the world of sense experience and personal history: this story is very informally based on the later life of the famous American philosopher Charles Sanders Peirce. Of course it is entirely fiction.

Q. Are there any of your stories in which escape or humor, rather than interpretation or revelation, dominates?

A. I have written a number of satiric stories set in a fictitious university, gathered in the collection *The Hungry Ghosts*. These are serious stories, too, but their structure, pace, and characterizations mark them as deliberately light or humorous reading.

Q. Which is your favorite of your stories?

A. A very difficult question to answer. "Queen of the Night," which appeared in a special limited edition (Lord John Press, 1979), is one of my favorites. I am extremely fond of "Daisy," too, and "Stalking" and "The Dead" from *Marriages and Infidelities;* and "In The Region

of Ice," "Where Are You Going, Where Have You Been?" and "How
I Contemplated the World from the Detroit House of Correction . . . "
from *The Wheel of Love.* "Famine Country" and "The Widows"
(which I recently expanded into a play) from *Night-Side* are additional favorites.

A final comment on discursive conversations: as Nietzsche warns,
"Talking much about oneself may be a way of hiding oneself." The
most reliable introduction to any writer is simply the books.

A Taste of Oates
Jay Parini/1983

From *Horizon*, November-December 1983. © 1983 Horizon
Publishers. Reprinted by permission.

"I hardly see myself as being unusual," says Joyce Carol Oates, who
at forty-five is one of America's most eminent writers of fiction. "I
take my writing seriously, but I don't take myself seriously . . . that is,
I don't feel pontifical or dogmatic. Writing is an absolutely fascinating
activity, an immersion in drama, language, and vision."

Such modesty provides a dazzling contrast to her achievements,
which include thirteen well-known novels, a dozen books of short
stories (which many critics think are her best work), several plays,
four remarkable collections of essays on a wide range of literary and
cultural topics, and five poetry books. Her novel *them* (1969)
received a National Book Award, and two others were nominated for
that award. Her stories have often won the prestigious O. Henry
Award, and she has been elected to the American Academy and
Institute of Arts and Letters. Critic Robert H. Fossum said: "Oates
may be the finest American novelist, man or woman, since Faulkner
. . . "—an extreme statement, perhaps, but a sentiment shared to
some extent by dozens of other critics since her first book of stories,
By the North Gate, was published in 1963.

This month Oates will publish her fourteenth novel, *Mysteries of
Winterthurn,* a complex tale of murder and the pursuit of love. The
novel's hero is Xavier Kilgarven, an idealistic and glamorous detective
who, in the course of this five-hundred-plus-page story, solves three
exotic cases at decade intervals. Each case, in typical Oates fashion,
involves bizarre twists, some violence, and unnerving consequences.
In the midst of this, Kilgarven also manages to fall in love with his
beautiful and intriguing half-cousin, Perdita. Their love affair forms a
counterplot to the detective story, which all takes place in the myth-
ical town of Winterthurn during the latter part of the last century.
Oates herself elaborates: "This is the third in a quartet of novels that
have to do with American themes and settings and are meant to be

119

slightly parodistic, but at the same time altogether serious as novels. The fourth novel, *The Crosswicks Horror* [set in Princeton in 1905 and 1906, when Woodrow Wilson was president of the university] will be published in 1985." As usual, Oates writes on a grand scale; ambitious and productive.

As one might expect, any writer so prolific and so highly touted in general is likely to catch a good deal of harsh criticism, too; this seems especially true of Oates, whose hallucinatory and emotionally charged fiction disturbs many readers. Even her award-winning *them* elicited this remark from *Newsweek:* "This novel is a charnel house of Gothic paraphernalia: blood, fire, insanity, anarchy, lust, corruption, death by bullets, death by cancer, death by plane crash, death by stabbing, beatings, crime, riot, and even unhappiness." The London *Times Literary Supplement* snidely suggested that her novel *Wonderland* (1971) was aimed for "the sensation-mongering American market." A *Time* review of *The Assassins* (1975) referred to "the somewhat too prodigious Joyce Carol Oates." A percentage of reviewers has consistently been offended by Oates's industry and her use of violent subject matter, which includes her tendency to portray characters in states of mental extremity bordering on madness.

To these charges, Oates maintains a cool response. "Productivity is a relative matter," she says. "It's really insignificant. What is ultimately important is a writer's strongest books." As to the violence in her writing, she says, "Given the number of pages I've written, and then the 'violent' incidents dispersed throughout them, I rather doubt that I am a violent writer in any meaningful sense of the word." One does encounter numerous horrifying scenes in Oates's fiction, but her art is, as the saying goes, a mirror held up to life.

In person, Oates is warm, open, and generous. Tall and sylphlike, she has been described as "haunting" by many interviewers. Her striking black hair accents a face with large eyes and unusual features. According to her friend, Robert Phillips, "she is not photogenic; no photo has ever done justice to her appearance, which conveys grace and high intelligence." Her soft voice and courteous manners have sometimes been mistaken for aloofness. She avoids publicity and dislikes the personality cults that grow up around writers. Her immense output of books has attracted thousands of reviews and plenty of media attention, but Oates has been remarkably successful in keeping her personal life private.

She lives several miles outside of Princeton, New Jersey, with her husband Raymond Smith, who edits *The Ontario Review* and a special line of books from their home. They work from nearly adjacent offices in their home, which is a beautiful, glass-walled contemporary in a secluded area. Woods surround their house, which looks out onto a private pond; inside, the house is built around an atrium, conveying an atmosphere of greenery.

A professor at Princeton, Oates teaches literature with great gusto, according to her colleagues and former students. "I love teaching," she says. "I don't think I could do without it." It's not money that draws her to teaching; her recent novel *Bellefleur* (1980) has sold a million copies to date. "Teaching organizes my day," Oates explains. "I like to write in the morning and teach in the afternoons—the balance is right. It creates a rhythm for working."

Oates grew up in rural New York, near Lockport, the region of Erie County depicted in her early fiction as Eden County. Her grandfather was a steelworker, her father a tool-and-die designer. She attended a one-room school-house as a child, had few luxuries in growing up, and was the first person in her family to go to college. "We never thought she'd be *this* successful," says her father, Frederic Oates. "The turning point came when she won that short-story contest at *Mademoiselle*. She was still in college. Everything just took off from there." Her mother, Carolina Oates, traces her daughter's rise to fame back to childhood. "She was always so hardworking . . . a perfectionist at everything."

During her graduate-school studies at the University of Wisconsin, Oates met Raymond Smith, a student in the same department, and they married in 1961. Oates received her M.A. in English from Wisconsin and expected to continue for a Ph.D. She was just beginning her doctoral work at Rice, in Texas, when one of her short stories appeared on the honor roll of *Best American Short Stories*. She decided to abandon the Ph.D. for fiction—a decision she has never regretted. In 1962, the young couple moved to Detroit, where they both taught at the university. Living through tempestuous years in that city inspired *them,* Oates's biggest early success.

In 1967, the University of Windsor offered Smith and Oates jobs on their faculty, so they moved to Ontario, Canada, where they lived for more than a decade. During this enormously productive time, Oates published twenty-seven books, including six full-length novels. She and her husband moved to Princeton in 1978, completing a migratory pattern that is not uncommon in academic circles. Having come back to the northeastern section of the United States, Oates was, in effect, "home." Her novel *Son of the Morning* appeared just as she arrived at her new job, and five other novels followed quickly.

Bellefleur is the most prominent of these. Consider one brief paragraph in this novel—a taste of Oates.

> High in the mountains the seasons sped swiftly. Now the planet tipped north, now south. Now aurora borealis flooded the night sky and pitched into drunkenness all who gazed upon it; now all light was black—utterly and wordlessly black, as if eclipsed by the deep mire of man's sin.

Oates's well of creativity remains a mystery to her. "Whenever I finish a novel," she says, "I am certain that I have put literally everything I know into it—all of my feeling, my energy, my life—and that I can't possibly write another. Yet I continue to assemble notes, filling folders gradually, writing up sketches, little scenes, etcetera. If I'm thwarted in beginning a novel, as I often am—I was with *Bellefleur* for several years, also *Mysteries of Winterthurn,* which was devilishly difficult to think through—I write other, shorter things like poetry, short stories, essays. I've written entire novels—*Unholy Loves* was one—because I seemed to be blocked in writing a larger, more ambitious novel."

In her art as in her life, Oates has created a special preserve all her own, though not disconnected from America as we move to the close of this century. Her glass house near Princeton—with its mallard ducks floating in the pond, its deer and raccoons creeping up to the house—is as fragile as it looks. Oates knows this, and she knows, too, that nothing survives of us on this planet but our imaginings. "Life is energy, and energy is creativity," she says. "And even when we as individuals pass on, the energy is retained in the work of art, locked in it and awaiting release if only someone will take the time and the care to unlock it."

A Conversation with Joyce Carol Oates

Frank McLaughlin/1985

From *Writing!*, September 1985 21-23. © September 1985 *Writing!* Reprinted by permission.

Joyce Carol Oates began creating fictional worlds when she was in elementary school. She submitted her first novel to a publisher when she was fifteen. It was rejected as being too depressing for young readers.

Like most writers, she became deeply absorbed in the imaginative worlds of other authors. While studying at Syracuse University, she was "Frank Kafka for a while." Faulkner, Nietzsche, Dostoyevski, Melville, and a host of other writers also were influences. Her short story, "In the Old World," won the *Mademoiselle* college fiction award in 1959. After graduating with her B.A., she entered the University of Wisconsin to pursue a graduate degree. She met and married Raymond Smith there. Oates followed her husband to Texas where he taught and she planned to work on a doctorate. While browsing in the library at Rice University, she found that one of her short stories had been cited in the honor role of a volume of *Best American Short Stories.* She decided that she could be a writer.

Joyce Carol Oates published her first novel, *With Shuddering Fall,* in 1964. Since then she has been indefatigable.

Readers of *Writing!* might especially find her book, *First Person Singular: Writers on Their Craft,* rewarding. Available in paperback from Persea Books, it is a collection featuring twenty-nine American writers talking about their work.

Joyce Carol Oates tries "to create the psychological and emotional equivalent of an experience, so completely and in such exhaustive detail, that anyone who reads it sympathetically will have experienced that event in his mind. . . . " There are very few segments of the American landscape she does not touch. Her most recent novel, *Solstice,* aptly demonstrates her penetrating insight into obsessive relationships. It vividly chronicles the volatile friendship of two very different women.

Frank McLaughlin: *Did you set out to become a writer or did you gravitate toward writing?*

Joyce Carol Oates: Virtually all children are creative—telling stories, singing, dancing, drawing, etc. Some children simply continue with one or another of these activities, and I was evidently one of them. I've always been "writing"—telling stories in various ways— even drawing stories before I knew how to write. Interviewers ask me about this phase of my life as if it were something extraordinary, but I persist in thinking it was all very ordinary, natural. I've been telling stories all my life, though I will admit that they have increased a good deal in complexity and ambiguity and ambition.

McLaughlin: *What was the one-room schoolhouse like that you attended as a child? Do you think your schooling offered any advantage over schools today?*

Oates: It was a single-room rural schoolhouse in southern Niagara County on the bank of the Tonawanda Creek in Millersport, New York—a fairly modest woodframe building razed some years ago. There were eight grades in the school, taught by one teacher. Now such single-room schools are highly unusual, at least in the Northeast, but at that time—in the 1940s—they were fairly common.

Yes, I think I did have some advantage, if by "advantage" one means stimulation of various kinds, not always or exclusively intellectual. This was a rough, unsentimental world that taught me a good deal about life. How our teacher, Mrs. Dietz, managed in these circumstances I can't guess. At the time she seemed quite confident, and she was certainly a strong-willed woman—but, looking back, I can see she must have had some extremely difficult days.

McLaughlin: *Were you a reader as a child? What were your most memorable books?*

Oates: Yes, I read a good deal. *Alice in Wonderland* and *Alice's Adventures through the Looking-Glass* were my most important books.

McLaughlin: *What prompted you to major in English at Syracuse University? Did you take courses with any writers there? Was there a professor who recognized your talent? Encouraged you?*

Oates: I majored in English for the reason that I loved literature; I minored in philosophy. I took no courses with writers, but there were a number of excellent professors at Syracuse with whom I studied— Walter Sutton and Donald Dike come immediately to mind. But everyone encouraged me; I was always extremely fortunate. Nor did I encounter any evident discrimination against me because of my sex.

McLaughlin: *To write and publish as much as you have—novels, poetry, short stories, essays, sometimes as many as two or three books a year—I would imagine you have a regimen. Where and when do you write?*

Oates: I haven't really written "two or three" books a year. Some titles listed in my bibliography are only short stories or a small grouping of poems published as limited editions. So this is mis-leading. Of course I have a regimen, like everyone I know. I work in the mornings from about eight until one; then again from four to seven. Sometimes I work in longhand in the evening. But I try never to push myself since I believe that writing (like reading) should be primarily enjoyable, a relaxation of the soul. (On teaching days—Mondays and Wednesdays—naturally this schedule is altered. I teach in the afternoon.)

McLaughlin: *How do you balance writing and teaching? Does your teaching help you as a writer?*

Oates: I've very rarely written about teaching—it's a wonderful activity but extremely difficult to make interesting. I don't, in fact, think that teaching helps me as a writer except very generally: we talk in my workshops about revision, "careful" writing, use of language, imagery, and proper grammar. But I suppose I would be well aware of these elements whether I taught or not.

I like teaching because I like my students: perhaps it's as simple as that.

McLaughlin: *Your novel* them *[winner of the National Book Award] was written while you taught at the University of Detroit. Did that novel grow out of the turmoil, the riots you witnessed then?*

Oates: Yes. Moving to Detroit in the early 1960s changed my life completely. I would have been a writer—my first book had already been accepted for publication, in fact, when I was twenty-three. But living in Detroit, enduring the extraordinary racial tensions of that city, and, indeed, living only a few blocks from some of the looting and burning of the summer of 1967, made me want to write directly about the serious social concerns of our time. I wanted to write about individuals who were also participants in a vast social drama—the complexity (and the tragedy) of which they barely grasped.

McLaughlin: *Would you share with us how you got the idea for one of your stories?*

Oates: The idea for the first mystery of *Mysteries of Winterthurn* began when I read about an elderly woman in Pennsylvania who had died alone after having been a recluse for many years. When her house was opened and searched, several mummified infants were found in her attic, having been strangled. The woman had been a spinster. I thought about the situation for a long time, off and on, imagining that household—"haunted," in a sense, by the murdered babies in the attic. And finally I wrote a mystery-detective novel in which the babies get their revenge.

McLaughlin: *May Sarton says that she writes novels to have a dialogue with other people. She notes, "Every one of my novels has been written to answer a question, not to tell people something, but to find out what I really think or feel." Is your approach similar?*

Oates: Yes, this is true of all writers. Though there is far more to it than that—what "I think or feel" is a small part of a large ambitious novel, after all. I do a good deal of research and am not content with simply writing about things from my own limited perspective.

McLaughlin: *Do your peers influence you? Do you read as much now as you did before? Do you read differently now?*

Oates: I think "influence" is general, ubiquitous. Sometimes we are as powerfully influenced by a mere anecdote or tale told to us by another writer. Yes, I probably read about as much as ever. I'm always reading two or three books at a time, usually fiction, non-fiction, perhaps poetry.

McLaughlin: *During the past five years you have been experimenting with different fictional forms. Are you more interested in experimenting with narrative techniques/voices or do these forms allow you new ways to explore consciousness?*

Oates: It interests me immensely that in writing a "mystery-detective" novel, one begins to see the world in terms of mystery. And the world *is* infinitely mysterious. If one writes a romance (even a post-modernist romance like *A Bloodsmoor Romance*), one begins to see the world in romantic terms. My central concern, however, is with American history and on-going American society, so my subject matter does, in a sense, take precedence over the experimentation. I'm not at all interested in experimentation for its own sake.

McLaughlin: *As you reflect on the vision you started with, and then consider how the work turned out, which book are you most satisfied with?*

Oates: Since it was the most difficult novel to write, and the most ingenious in its plotting, *Mysteries of Winterthurn* is my favorite. I am psychologically very close to the detective hero, Xavier Kilgarven (allowing of course for fictional differences).

McLaughlin: *You have won many awards, honors, and critical accolades. What motivates you to continue writing?*

Oates: Very likely the same impulse that motivated me at the start. (But these impulses are extremely mysterious . . .)

McLaughlin: *Could you tell us something about what you are working on now?*

Oates: My next novel, which I am completing at the present time, is titled *Marya: A Life*. It's the rather rough coming-of-age of a young woman whose life, in some respects, parallels my own and is, in others, completely different. It will be published in February 1986 by Dutton. Almost without my intending it, *Marya* moved toward a "happy" ending.

My Friend, Joyce Carol Oates: An Intimate Portrait

Elaine Showalter/1986

From *Ms. Magazine*, March 1986 44-50. © 1986 *Ms. Magazine*. Reprinted by permission.

For a serious American writer—especially for "a woman writer," Joyce Carol Oates told an interviewer in 1980, "this is by far the best era in which to live." Certainly the 1980s have seen the extraordinary flowering of Oates's protean talent. This year has already seen the publication of a new novel, and her classic short story about female adolescence, "Where Are You Going, Where Have You Been?" has been made into a sensitive film, "Smooth Talk," by the feminist director Joyce Chopra (see *Ms.*, February, 1986). Yet despite her position as one of the most versatile and intellectually powerful of contemporary American writers, and despite the series of important books on female experience she has written especially during this decade, Oates has never had the acknowledgment from feminist readers and critics that she deserves.

Her newest and most intensely moving novel, *Marya: A Life,* published last month by Dutton, may change this pattern. It is a wrenching account of the development of a woman writer who reaches back to the wasteland of her brutal childhood to find the mother who has abandoned her, and to reclaim a matrilineage that is both painful and empowering. *Marya,* which insists on the woman writer's need to confront her female inheritance and to seek the lost mother although she may be as disturbing as she is comforting, is Oates's most personal statement about a female literary tradition, as well as the novel which presents her most compelling heroine.

In writing about Joyce Carol Oates, one must inevitably deal with the two issues that every critical discussion of her work has mentioned for 20 years: its "quantity" and its "violence." She is indeed extraordinarily productive. Since 1964, when her first book appeared, Oates has published 17 novels, 13 volumes of short stories, eight collections of poetry, five books of literary criticism, and two

128

books of plays. Hundreds of her short stories are still uncollected, and there are enough unpublished novels waiting in her desk drawer to take her through the 1990s. This is an impressive record, although many Victorian novelists, for example, equaled or surpassed it (Anthony Trollope wrote 46 novels, even George Gissing, that hardluck case, 27); but for a woman writer, critics have hinted, such fecundity is positively indecent. One fierce novel and consumption, or obscurity and a post-humous trunkful of poems in the attic, seem more decorous for someone who is, after all, a *serious* writer. Some criticism is plainly envious; Oates herself has noted that "perhaps critics (mainly male) who charged me with writing too much are secretly afraid that someone will accuse them of having done too little with their lives."

How does she do it? Oates leads a balanced but intensely disciplined life, in which writing comes first. She lives with her husband of 25 years, the editor and critic Raymond Smith, in a bright country house near Princeton University, where she has been a Lecturer in Creative Writing since 1978. She gets up very early, and stays up rather late, and writes for several hours every day, most recently on a new IBM computer, which, she says, feels like an extension of her brain waves.

Yet there is room in her life for other pleasures. She is sociable and athletic, finding time in addition to her teaching and writing for a daily run in the woods, and for gossipy lunches and long phone conversations with a wide circle of women friends around Princeton and New York (including novelist and film writer Eleanor Bergstein, the poet Alicia Ostriker, lawyer Leigh Bienen, to whom *Marya* is dedicated, journalist Lucinda Franks, and Princeton colleagues Sandra Gilbert and myself).

She keeps up a huge correspondence with fellow writers, both men and women; serves on numerous committees for literature and the arts; and is a frequent traveler and speaker on college campuses. She also does her own housework and occasionally jokes that she will volunteer to wash windows for less organized friends.

She does not, however, suffer fools or bores glady, send Christmas cards, bake or indeed eat cookies, or go shopping for clothes (I once persuaded her to come with me to a discount fashion store, a successful expedition during which she added a red mohair coat to a wardrobe of clothes made and regularly mailed from Millersport, New York, by her mother). Yet to say these things makes her sound like any successful woman executive of the 1980s, and she is most decidedly not like other people. In the midst of a quite ordinary conversation about the news or television or the family, Oates often inserts remarks whose philosophical penetration makes the rest of us feel like amoebas in the company of a more highly evolved life form. She seems to be someone who is never blocked, whose unconscious is always available, who is most alive when she is writing and working. She has the uncanny personal power of genius.

In the 1970s, Oates's work was often criticized for its violent themes and images, for scenes of riots, beatings, and murders; and reviewers wondered whether some trauma of her own was responsible for her dark vision. Oates responded in an 1981 essay for the *New York Times Book Review,* called "Why Is Your Writing So Violent?" The question, she wrote, was "always insulting . . . ignorant . . . always sexist," a question that would never be asked of a serious male artist. It came from the belief that women should limit their writing to the domestic and the subjective; that in a violent society and century, "war, rape, murder, and the more colorful minor crimes evidently fall within the exclusive province of the male writer, just as, generally, they fall within the exclusive province of male action."

In the early years of Oates's career (and recently in the aftermath of her much-publicized essay on boxing for the *New York Times Magazine*), critical shock at her violent imagination was often accompanied by surprise at her feminine appearance: could this delicate creature be the author of these powerful stories? Walter Clemons's comments in *Newsweek* are typical of the genre: "If you met her at a literary party and failed to catch her name, it might be hard to imagine her reading, much less writing, the unflinching fiction [of Joyce Carol Oates]." In the 19th century, women who wrote sensational fiction under pseudonyms, such as Rhoda Broughton, were sometimes forbidden by their fathers to read their own books.

Oates is not particularly gentle, as it happens; she is fast and tough, funny and outspoken, impatient with pomposity and cant. But it's not simply a question of getting her right, or of asking the *real* "Joyce Carol Oates" to stand up. Just as her name exists only for the title

page of books (nobody calls her "Joyce Carol"), she has always
insisted that the writer exists only in words, and that the contrast
between the printed self—"revised tirelessly, monomaniacally . . . so
that it is as close to perfection as possible"—and the private self—
"mere flesh"—must always be disappointing. Oates has maintained
that, for the woman writer, this split between the private and public
identities must be even greater, since "when the writer is alone . . .
with language," she experiences herself as genderless. Yet she has
also acknowledged that the woman who writes "is a woman writer by
others' definitions." Her appearance, her femininity, her conformity
to a sexual identity that is socially defined, must be part of the world
in which her work is judged.

Feminist critics have sometimes taken Oates's insistence that the
imagination has no gender as a denial of her social identity as a
woman writer, yet Oates's sense of herself as what she calls a
"(woman) writer" has intensified during the 1980s. It is not that she
has abandoned or in any way simplified the complex intellectual
allegiances to philosophy or classic literature that mark her writing,
but that she has added to it an exchange with an equally complex
female literary heritage. Oates's early relationship to the male literary
tradition is most clearly presented in her book of short stories,
Marriages and Infidelities (1972), in which she brilliantly reimagines
and rewrites famous stories by Chekhov, Kafka, James, Joyce, and
others. In an interview with Joe David Bellamy, Oates has explained
that "these stories are meant to be autonomous stories, yet they are
also testaments of my love and extreme devotion to these other
writers; I imagine a kind of spiritual 'marriage' between myself and
them."

Yet even within these literary "marriages" were the signs of
infidelities: betrayals of theme, transgressions of form, transforming
revisions of perspective that came from female experience. One story,
"The Dead," is about the breakdown of Ilena Williams, a successful
young novelist and teacher, whose anxiety, insomnia, and anorexia
seem to signal her dis-ease with the male institutions of the university,
marriage, and literature.

These signs of rebellion and subversion within a framework of
wifely devotion and service to a patriarchal tradition take on added
meaning in the light of Oates's work since 1980, much of which has

been a meditation, from a dazzling variety of perspectives, on female creativity and female community. Her virtuoso fictional trilogy, *Belle-fleur* (1980), *A Bloodsmoor Romance* (1982), and *Mysteries of Winterthurn* (1984), experiments with the female genres of the family chronicle, the romance, and the gothic. All explore what Oates has called the "on-going wrongs of women," from arranged marriages and domestic confinement to rape, sexual abuse, and incest. These novels also forge a bold alliance of male and female literary traditions, juxtaposing epigraphs and conventions from Louisa May Alcott, Emily Brontë, and Emily Dickinson, with those from Thoreau and Hawthorne.

In *Bloodsmoor,* a woman medium, "Deirdre of the Shadows," possessed by voices from the spirit world which she must translate, is Oates's representation of her own creative process. In *Mysteries of Winterthurn,* Oates invents both the character and the poems of a 19th-century woman writer much like Emily Dickinson, called "Iphigenia," and suggests through her narrative how much this woman, like her contemporaries, was sacrificed to patriarchal tyranny. While the novels satirically explore the more grandiose and blood-thirsty manifestations of patriarchal power, such as lynching, assassination, and nuclear weapons, they also suggest, through their interplay of "masculine" and "feminine" narrative conventions, how the plots and fantasies of the novel genre itself have invidiously wronged women.

In *Solstice* (1985), Oates turned away from these long historical novels to a brief chilling study of the relationship between two women. Utterly without sentimentality about female friendships, *Solstice* shows how the balance of power between the two women— one a famous painter, the other a teacher—is never resolved. Oates tells the story through the teacher, the weaker of the two, so that the artist remains always remote, inexplicable, frighteningly seductive, and dangerous. Without avoiding the erotic tension that bonds the women in sexual games and that drives each close to sickness and breakdown, Oates concentrates more on the drive for possession and dominance, the illusion of equality, in any love relationship.

Marya: A Life seems to bring these two strands of Oates's thought on the female tradition together. The heroine, Marya Knauer, is a brilliant writer who has been hurt and betrayed by both women and

men. She is abandoned by her sluttish mother after her miner father's
death when she is eight years old, an experience she will try to forget
yet endlessly relive in dreams and in adult configurations of love and
loss. She grows up with working-class relatives in the country along
the Canal Road, where there are strange wild landscapes: the
mother's wilderness, "nine miles of unpaved dirt and gravel . . . lush-
growing scrub willow and oak and beech; the roadside wildflowers,
chicory and Queen Anne's lace; patches of milkweed; poison ivy;
pink sweetpeas"; and the father's wonderland of wrecked cars. Both
are tempting and dangerous, but most of all the mother's world,
where even the lacy flower "was nasty, the tiny black dot at the
center, you'd think it was an insect or something."

Growing up female, smart, and wary in an environment where the
female and the intelligent are natural victims, Marya struggles to
destroy everything in her that bears the mother's mark, the mark of
the body, of sexuality, of vulnerability. Sexually abused by her loutish
cousin, mocked and harassed by the village toughs, she learns to
close off her body, to become "not-there," and to deny her own
desires for intimacy and touch. In high school, she thinks of
becoming a nun. Yet the short stories she hesitantly begins to write
frighten her. She dreads looking into the mirror and seeing "something forbidden: her mother's face, that slack-lidded wink, the glassy
stare, the smile rimmed with lipstick and saliva," the heavy hair "like
her own mother's hair."

The night before Marya leaves home for the university where she
alone has won a scholarship, her waist-length hair—the mother's
mark—is cut off by her drunken and envious classmates in a scene
that is both a kind of rape and a rite of passage. In adulthood, as she
becomes a successful professor and writer—the novel takes her to the
age of 36—she is a woman who is trying to be genderless, to deny
the body and live in and through the mind. But every intellectual
advance intensifies Marya's sense of estrangement. Unable to
acknowledge the intensity of her longing for female affection, Marya
helplessly repeats the patterns of her childhod, in affairs with older
married men, who die and leave her abandoned but somehow
connected to their wives, the lost "mothers" with whom she has
unconsciously bonded.

Oates never idealizes the process by which Marya comes to the decision that at mid-life she must reclaim a matrilineal past. The community of women is not idyllic, but torn by rage, competition, primal jealousies, ambiguous desire, and emotional violence, just like the world in which women seem subordinate to and victimized by men. And we do not know what kind of renewal Marya's reunion with her mother will bring. The novel ends with Marya holding up the letter and the snapshot of the mother whose reappearance will "cut [her] life in two." This intensely moving conclusion may remind some readers of the famous freeze-frame at the end of Truffaut's "400 Blows," in which the autobiographical young hero on the run comes to the sea and stops, with nowhere else to go; except that for Oates's heroine the final frame is a powerful moment of opening rather than confinement. The mother's country may be a wilderness rather than a peaceful or paradisal garden; yet to refuse or to deny it is to be in permanent exile.

Joyce Carol Oates and the Hardest Part of Writing

Michael Schumacher/1986

From *Writer's Digest*, April 1986, 30-34. © 1986 *Writer's Digest*. Reprinted by permission.

Joyce Carol Oates has come to typify the writer-as-artist. Shying away from interviews and public appearances, she prefers instead to work privately at her craft and teach her skills to others. Though the sheer bulk of her creative output seems to deny it, she revises her work tirelessly, rearranging words and passages—even titles of stories—to achieve their designed effects; on one occasion, she changed the entire ending of a novel between the time it was published in America and in England. Her idea of taking a break from the tension of writing novels is to write poetry or short stories.

When her first collection of short stories, *By the North Gate*, was published in 1963, few observers would have predicated that the quietly intense young woman from rural New York would develop into one of America's most prolific serious writers. Between then and now, Oates has published 16 novels, 12 story collections, five volumes of poetry and four books of literary essays, as well as plays and countless uncollected book reviews and short stories. *Prodigious* is an adjective often associated with her creative output, and her publishing history indicates the term is appropriate: at one point, she had three publishers— one handling her mainstream writings, another her poetry, and the third her experimental work. At age 46, Oates shows no sign of slowing down.

Reaction to her work has always been mixed, though generally favorable. As a college student, she submitted a short story to a *Mademoiselle* competition and won; in 1970, she won the National Book Award for *them*, a novel set in Detroit, her home for six years in the mid '60s. Her short stories are staples in the O. Henry and similar anthologies of award-winning pieces. Her work is studied on college campuses throughout the United States, in both literature and creative writing classes. One of her most recent novels, *Bellefleur*, sold more than a million copies and reached hardcover and paperback bestseller lists. She is a member of the American Academy of Arts and Letters.

Criticism of her work has mounted over the years, however; hostile reviewers dismiss her recent string of Gothic and romance genre novels as inappropriate or disappointing from a novelist who has proven herself so adept at contemporary themes. Her books have been assailed as too violent. Some critics have gone as far as to disapprove of the *number* of books she has written. It has been pointed out, to her displeasure, that she fails to "write like a woman"—whatever that means.

Though far from insensitive to critical reaction, positive *or* negative, she dismisses it with good humor: "I've never taken it very seriously, since for me the hard part of writing is the writing, not the critical response afterward. Conversely, the writer wishes that good, strong, positive reviews had the power to convince him or her that the writing *is* successful. As John Updike has wryly said, we tend to believe the worst, and to think that the good reviews have simply been kind."

By all indications, Joyce Carol Oates is living a life rich enough for several people. In addition to her writing, she teaches at Princeton University, co-edits (with her husband, Raymond Smith) a literary quarterly, and publishes small-press books; for recreation, she enjoys cooking, jogging, bicycling, playing classical music on the piano, reading, and taking brief excursions to nearby New York City. She admits, though, that little of what she does takes her very far from her writing and conversely, that almost everything she does is somewhat connnected to her work.

"My life is a sort of double narrative," she says—"*my* life running alongside an interior/fictional life. The external life is often absorbing in itself, particularly here at Princeton, but the internal life is ultimately the one that endures. I do subordinate nearly everything else in life to my writing— that is, the thinking about the story at hand. But this may well be simply analogous to the degree of saturation in thought—of self or others or of various projects—common to all human beings."

"Telling stories, I discovered at the age of three or four, is a way of being told stories," she wrote in a *New York Times* essay. "One picture yields another; one set of words, another set of words. Like our dreams, the stories we tell are also the stories we are told." Born the daughter of a tool-and-die designer in the tiny town of Millersport in New York's Erie County, Oates recalls her rural upbringing as "a continual daily scramble for existence," frequently marred by her being bullied by older schoolmates. Storytelling became an important escape and she credits her paternal grandfather, a steelworker, as a great early influence. Not only did he delight her with stories, which she tried to emulate, but he bought her her first typewriter when she turned 14.

Her short stories appeared in small literary quarterlies while she pursued academic degrees in English, but when she read a publisher's ad seeking young writers, she set aside her academic life and began pursuing her writing fulltime. "After my first publication," she told *Publishers Weekly*, "I immersed myself in writing for 12 to 16 hours a day. Writing became the core of my life."

When I ask if she could have done something other than write, she replies: "It seems to me in retrospect that I could not have done anything else, but the impulse to romanticize oneself is obviously dominant."

Writer's Digest: In a recent interview, you mentioned that you don't write for everybody, and that you don't expect everyone to read you. Who do you write for?

Oates: This is a difficult question to answer. I doubt that any *serious* writer thinks of an audience while he or she is writing. My primary area of challenge—or tension, or at times anxiety—is simply the work at hand, the next morning's provisionary and often endlessly revised and retyped scene. In structuring a novel, I have a quite detailed outline—even an "architectural" sort of design affixed to my wall—but as each chapter or scene is written, the whole design is altered. So I am in a constant state of tension while writing a first draft, as I am at the present time. Even the first draft is the consequence of what seems to be endless revisions of chapters, pages, even paragraphs. The primary focus of concentration is therefore the work at hand. To think of an audience—of anyone!— reading the material is virtually impossible. It's analogous to worrying about what you'll wear on the morning of March 10, 1988. One should live so long.

When the work is completed, however, one can make some sort of judgment, as editors and publishers do, about whether it is likely to be popular or not. I can't see my writing as ever being *popular*, much of it, to make even literal—not to mention emotional, psychological or thematic—sense, has to be reread. When *Bellefleur* became a bestseller in both hardcover and paperback, no one was more surprised than I was, but I'm sure that many of the copies sold went unread or unfinished. For this, a writer does feel some slight guilt, I think, and hence my statement that I really *don't* see myself as writing for a very large audience.

WD: Over the years, you've addressed a number of critical attacks concerning the violence in your work, yet I can't help but wonder if there's a gender identification connected with the criticism: If Norman Mailer writes about a man finding the severed head of a woman, it's macho artform; if you write a novel about a boy who murders his mother, or a novel about the assassination of a politician, critics question your motives. It's as if women are expected to be "civil" (in the Austen sense of the word) and controlled.

Oates: Yes, it's purely a sexist response but I think it's beginning to diminish. In the past, it may well have seemed even to responsible critics that a woman's natural artform was needlework; hence, any deviation from this genteel activity was alarming. I did draw a good deal of angry abuse—"sickening," "loathsome," "disgusting," "mere trash"—and perhaps I still do. I've never taken it seriously.

WD: Did you read Mailer's *Tough Guys Don't Dance*? Though the book is contemporary, it seems familiar with much of what you were doing in *Mysteries of Winterthurn*. Both books seemed to be working to establish correlations and contrasts related to physical and psychological violence.

Oates: I haven't read Mailer's novel yet, but I would suspect that Mailer and I have many concerns or obsessions in common. However, the relationship between physical and psychological violence is one fairly generally explored, isn't it? I know I have been exploring it since my first published stories.

WD: About *Mysteries of Winterthurn*: You've said that book taught you a new way of writing. What did you mean by that?

Oates: The detective-mystery novel must be imagined both forward and backward. Unlike most novels—most serious novels, in any case—this peculiar and highly challenging genre demands absolute accuracy in terms of time, place, details, clues, etc. I realize, of course, that in conventional detective-mysteries the plot is all, or nearly all, but my concern was with writing a "double" novel in a sense, a novel of character and theme that nonetheless required the classic structure of the mystery. The novel I have written, however, is in fact an anti-detective-mystery, a critique of the genre from the inside. As I grew to love the form, I grew to realize the strange nature of its restrictions and its many necessary exclusions—as in, for instance, a game of chess one must abide by the rules and take for granted that the world "beyond" the game board scarcely exists, in fact does *not* exist. Otherwise the game is jeopardized.

WD: That book, as well as the other period pieces you've written recently, not only recreated the times but was also authentic in duplicating the writing style of the day. How did you research this? Did you read a lot of 19th-century Gothic novels?

Oates: I've done a good deal of reading over the years, of course. But the 19th-century novel is immensely varied; what is meant by *Gothic*, in fact, is debatable. I read a number of novels by women writers of the mid and late 19th century. Susan Warner is the out-standing example. And etiquette books, handbooks on how to live—with such titles as *The Young Christian Wife and Mother*, which I discuss in *The Profane Art* in a long essay on stereotypical female images in Yeats, Lawrence, and Faulkner.

WD: You've worked in widely diverse styles in your stories and novels. The obvious question: Is style something that you can control, or do your stories dictate the way in which they are told?

Oates: It's a mysterious process. The character on the page determines the prose—its music, its rhythms, the range and limit of its vocabulary—yet, at the outset at least, I determine the character. It usually happens that the fictitious character, once released, acquires a life and will of his or her own, so the prose, too, acquires its own inexplicable fluidity. This is one of the reasons I write: to "hear" a voice not quite my own, yet summoned forth by way of my own.

WD: Your story collection *The Poisoned Kiss and Other Stories From the Portuguese* went as far as to name a fictional character as your "collaborator," giving the book a sort of visionary glow. Could you explain how that book came into being? Is this an example of what you mean when you say that writing is a transcendental function?

Oates: The appeal of writing—of any kind of *artistic* activity—is primarily the investigation of mystery. Somehow, by employing a deliberate speech-rhythm, or by unlocking it, one is able to follow a course into the psyche that reveals different facets of the self. *The Poisoned Kiss* is my journal of a sort of the most extreme experience of my own along these lines: Actually, I gave to the *voice* of the stories the adjective "Portuguese" because I knew only that it was foreign, yet not familiarly foreign. Beyond this, it is difficult to speak.

I should stress, though, that the *voice* of these tales was firmly joined to a fairly naturalistic setting by way of subsequent research and conversations with friends who knew Portugal well. And the tales were rigorously written and rewritten.

WD: Could you talk a little about revision? I understand that you spend a great deal of time reworking your novels and stories.

Oates: I revise endlessly, tirelessly—chapters, scenes, paragraphs . . . I don't like to push forward with a story or novel unless it seems to me that the prose is strong enough to be permanent, even though I know very well that once the work is finished I will want to rewrite it. The pleasure *is* the rewriting: The first sentence can't be written until the final sentence is written. This is a koan-like statement, and I don't mean to sound needlessly obscure or mysterious, but it's simply true. The completion of any work automatically necessitates its revisioning. The same is true with reading, of course—at least of a solid, serious, meticulously written work.

WD: How does a novice writer perfect revision skills?

Oates: Since we are all quite different, I can't presume to say. Rereading, with an objective eye, is a necessity—trying to *see* one's work as if it were the work of another, setting aside involvements of the ego. . . . Revision is in itself a kind of artwork, a process of discipline and refinement that has to be experienced. It cannot really be taught. But my students are amazed and excited by what they learn by revising; they're usually very grateful that they are "strongly encouraged" to do so.

WD: Is it possible to revise too much? Can one be too much of a perfectionist—such as the painter who keeps adding brush strokes to a canvas until the original picture and its inspiration are painted over or altered beyond recognition?

Oates: Certainly. Some people think that, on some pages at least, *Ulysses* is over-polished, its slender narrative heavily burdened with various layers of significance, symbol-motifs, allusions. I am temperamentally hostile to the weighting down of a natural and spontaneous story with self-conscious Significance: to me, the hard part of writing *is* the story. The gifts of a Thomas Hardy, for instance, are far more remarkable than the gifts of a writer like Malcolm Lowry, who so painfully and doggedly and willfully created a novel of symbols/ideas/Significance.

I admire Joyce immensely, of course; I've written a good deal about him. But he had the true Jesuitical mind—as he himself noted—plotting, calculating, outlining, dissecting: In *Portrait of the Artist as a Young Man*, Stephen experiences the "seven deadly sins" in a programmatic way, for instance; once one knows the key, the story seems willed, artificial, slightly tainted by the author's intention. It's ideal fiction for teaching, however.

WD: Where does your writing fit in?

Oates: Temperamentally, I may be more akin to Virginia Woolf, who worked very hard, as she noted in her diary, to achieve a surface of "fluidity, breathlessness, spontaneity." One wants the reader to *read* swiftly and with pleasure, perhaps even with some sense of suspense; one hardly wants the reader to pause and admire a symbol. In my genre novels, I had to use conspicuously big words since, to me, that is part of the quaint humor of 19th-century fiction—its humor and its power—but these are not my words, they are those of my narrators.

At the present time, I am writing a novel, set in the years 1947-1956, called *The Green Island*. My hope is to create a colloquial, fluid, swiftly moving prose that sounds, in places—when certain characters are on stage, for instance—rather rough, sheerly spontaneous. Yet I write and rewrite to achieve this "roughness." My prose tends to be more polished, to a degree, in its first state—at least more systematic and grammatical. To find the right voice for this novel, I have had to break down my own voice.

WD: You've drawn a distinction between ideal fiction for reading and ideal fiction for teaching. Have you, through your mainstream and experimental fiction, been seeking a compromise between the two?

Oates: Yes. I believe *every* writer wants to be read by as many people as possible—with the stress on *possible*. That is, one doesn't

want at all to modify his or her standards; there is the hope that
readers will make an effort, sympathize, try just a little harder, reread,
reconsider—the effort that is routinely made with Modernists like
Joyce and Yeats. Since I work so particularly hard on rewriting, and
can do a dozen versions of an opening section after I've completed a
novel to get it right or in harmony and proportion with the rest of the
book, it would seem that my opening sections should be reread, too.
Yet I doubt that many—any?—reviewers trouble to make the effort.
However, I do keep trying. I must be incurably optimistic.

WD: Did you ever find yourself beginning a story or novel which
was difficult or impossible to execute?

Oates: I have never begun a novel that hasn't been *impossible* for
the first six or more weeks. Seriously! The outset of a novel is sheer
hell and I dread beginning. But it must be done . . . I've written 100
pages or more to be thrown away in despair, but with the understanding that the pages had to be written in order that the first
halfway-good page might come forth. When I tell my students this,
they stare at me in pity and terror. When I tell them that my
published work is perhaps one half of the total work I've done—
counting apprentice work, for instance—they turn rather pale. They
can't seem to imagine such effort and, in retrospect, I must confess
that I can't, either. If I had to do it all over again, I'm not sure that I
could.

WD: Much of your prose has a rhythmic and lyrical quality about
it that approaches poetry. Do you consciously write for the mind's
ear? Do you ever read passages aloud to hear what they sound like?

Oates: Absolutely, all the time. It's a practice I am totally dependent on, and have grown to love, though I don't usually read the
passages out loud. *Silently out loud*, if that makes sense.

WD: Your use of ellipses, as well as your intermixing of short and
long paragraphs on the same page, makes me wonder if you work to
achieve a certain physical effect in your writing for the printed page.
Are you looking for something physical?

Oates: Sometimes—certainly in my poetry and in some short
stories. In *Childwold*, I had wanted varying spaces between the
chapters to suggest varying "spaces" in the narrative and between
characters, but my publisher didn't want to print the book that way.

WD: As it is, that was one of your most experimental major works.

Your use of the second-person singular was one of your most interesting experiments in language. How did you come to choose that particular way of telling that story? Was it a difficult book to write?

Oates: *Childwold* was written first, almost in its entirety, in longhand. When I finally began typing it, I think it went rather smoothly. The *you* seemed necessary for Laney because, though Laney was not *me/I*, she lived through and saw numerous things that I experienced at one time or another. Her focus of consciousness seemed to demand the second-person singular, which I don't believe I have ever used since.

WD: I felt a Faulkner or Flannery O'Connor influence in that novel. Do you find yourself influenced by certain writers when you're working? Do you ever go back and reread one of the classics in an effort to capture a particular flavor or style?

Oates: My reading is so wide, varied and idiosyncratic that it is impossible for me to say anything specific or helpful. I was reading Faulkner, Dostoevsky, Thoreau, Hemingway, the Brontës, and many other classic writers, in my early teens. These influences remain very deep, I'm sure. Only in my late teens and 20s did I read Lawrence, O'Connor, Thomas Mann, Kafka—yet these influences are still quite strong, pervasive. The curious thing, which I try to explain to my students, is that one can try very hard to be influenced but not succeed. Much of what we read is in a voice so alien to our own that there is no possibility of influence, though we might admire it a good deal. For instance, I *admire* Huxley, yet I could never have been influenced by him.

WD: Your books are filled with richly descriptive narrative passages. Do you keep notebooks or jot down ideas as you see them?

Oates: I do both, I suppose. For me, writing—and reading—are ways of *seeing*: I have a sharply visual imagination and love to see by way of words, and there are many writers (one might name Emily Brontë, Thomas Hardy and D.H. Lawrence) whose visual imaginations are so powerful that one is immediately transported to an alien but totally convincing world by way of their prose. Oddly, merely viewing without the filter of words, as in a film, seems to me less satisfying. I get a good deal of happiness out of transcribing scenes in retrospect, by way of memory—evoking the formidable city of Detroit, for instance, in *Do With Me What You Will*, while at the time I

was living in London, England, for a year; writing *Bellefleur*, set in
the mountains of a region very much like upstate New York, while
living in Princeton; and writing my current novel, *The Green Island*,
with a Buffalo/Lockport, New York, location, again while living in
Princeton. Conversely, I get no satisfaction out of writing about things
immediately at hand; they don't interest me at all. Part of the motive
for writing seems to me the act of conscious memory.

WD: A few questions about your writing habits: What is your daily
schedule like?

Oates: I try to begin work around 8 a.m., stop at 1 p.m., begin
again at 4 p.m., and work to perhaps 7 p.m. Sometimes, I will work
in the evening—in longhand, not at my desk—but throughout the
day I am *working* in my head so far as possible. This makes it sound
rather constant and perhaps it is, but the activity is rather more
exciting than tiring, at least when the story is moving along well. This
schedule is an ideal day when I am not at the university or involved
in other activities. Obviously, my two teaching days are radically
different: I'm gone through the afternoon.

WD: Do you still work in longhand?

Oates: Yes. I'm very dependent on working in longhand. All my
poetry and most of my novels are taken down in longhand first. It
seems close to the voice, more intimate, less formal and artificial.

WD: In what way? Could you explain that further?

Oates: I don't think I can, really. Most poets write in longhand;
even many of my students, who then turn to their word processors. I
am not averse to using the typewriter, of course, at certain more pragmatic times.

WD: How do you feel about word processors? It would seem ideal
for someone like you, who is usually involved in several projects at
once.

Oates: I am not usually involved in several projects at once; in
fact, when deep at work on a novel, I try to do very little else. My
short story writing has sharply abated in recent years since I've been
working on exceptionally long, complex novels.

The word processor isn't for me, since I am dependent on so many
systematic, slow, deliberate rewritings. Often I retype a page that
seems to me finally finished, only to discover in retyping that I've
tightened it, or added something that, in retrospect, seems obvious
and necessary.

WD: Can you talk about the different sorts of writing projects you undertake? Let's start with the short story. What role does the short story play in your activity as a writer?

Oates: I seem to have published more than 300 short stories since 1963, so their *role* is virtually indistinguishable from my life! Most obviously, the short story is a short run—a single idea and mood, usually no more than two or three characters, an abbreviated space of time. The short story lends itself most gracefully to experimentation, too. If you think about it, the story can't be defined, and hence is open, still in the making. Radical experimentation, which might be ill-advised in the novel, is well suited for the short story. I like the freedom and promise of the form.

WD: Do you find that, like a painter, you consciously work your stories into series of common themes or colors—such as in *Crossing the Border* and *Night-Side*—or do they sort of gather that way after a period of time?

Oates: Yes, I think the process is rather like that of a painter's: There are common concerns, common themes and obsessions, in a certain period of time. I collect only a few stories in proportion to the number I publish. To me, hardcover publication is the final imprimatur. When I assemble stories, as in *Last Days* and *A Sentimental Education*, my most recent collections, I rewrite them, at least in part, and arrange them in a specific order. My story collections are not at all mere collections; they are meant to be books, consciously organized. Unfortunately, a number of stories I am fond of have never found their way into hardcover print, because their themes or voices were unsuited for a volume.

WD: You've written a substantial amount of poetry—enough to merit a volume of collected poems. How does poetry fit into your life as a writer?

Oates: Poetry is my *other* world, my solace of a kind. I love both to read and to write—or to attempt to write—poetry as a means of escape from the strain of prose fiction. It is also an extremely personal mode for me, as fiction is not. I can employ autobiographical landscapes and even experiences in my fiction, but *I* never exist—there is no place for *I*.

In a phase of poetry writing, I feel that I am most at home in poetry. There is something truly enthralling about the process—the very finitude of the form, the opportunity for constant revision—an incantatory solace generally missing in fiction. Poetry requires no time in the reading as prose fiction always does, particularly the novel; the demands of the novel on both reader and writer are considerable, after all. After finishing a long, difficult novel, I always enter a phase of poetry. It can last for perhaps six or eight weeks. Of course, this phase is by no means without its own difficulties, but its pleasures are more immediate and forthcoming. One can even *see* a poem in its entirety—a source of amazement to the novelist.

WD: What about book reviews and literary essays? What function do they serve in your career?

Oates: I don't know that they serve any *function*; they are vehicles for my more discursive voice, I suppose. Like most critics, I write about what I like and hope to know more thoroughly by way of writing and analysis.

WD: One final question: If and when you write your memoirs, what period of your career would you consider to be your happiest?

Oates: I can't answer that—perhaps I don't yet have the perspective to make such a judgment. My husband and I are quite happy here in Princeton, and I've been extremely productive here, but I well remember feeling idyllic in Windsor, if not always in Detroit, where we lived from 1962 to 1968. Also, the concept of a *career* is rather foreign to me since a *career* is so outward, while *life* is so inward, a matter of daily experience. Many a writer has enjoyed an outwardly successful career while being personally unhappy, and the reverse might well be true. The most sustained and experimental—if not audacious—work of my career is the five-volume sequence of novels written here in Princeton. So I suppose this period, from 1978 onward, might be later seen as my "happiest" time.

A Sad Joyce Carol Oates Forswears Pseudonyms

Edwin McDowell/1987

Pronouncing herself surprised and very disappointed that her literary cover had been blown, Joyce Carol Oates said she would never again try to write a book under a pseudonym. She tried it this once, she said yesterday, because "I wanted to escape from my own identity."

The book is *Lives of the Twins*, a short psychological mystery supposedly written by Rosamond Smith. It is scheduled for publication in November by Simon & Schuster. The pseudonym is a feminization of the name of Miss Oates's husband, Raymond Smith, a publisher.

Miss Oates said she did not think it uncommon for a writer to write mysteries under a pseudonym. Nevertheless, her attempt at literary anonymity caused quite a stir when it became known yesterday. Among those bewildered by it were Blanche Gregory, Miss Oates's longtime literary agent, William Abrahams, her editor at E. P. Dutton, and Nancy Nicholas, the Simon & Schuster editor who signed *Lives of the Twins*.

"I don't know that I'm publishing Joyce Carol Oates," said Ms. Nicholas, who had not spoken with the author yesterday. "I signed *Lives of the Twins* in good faith as a first novel." Now, she said, she will have to talk with the agent, "find if it is, in fact, Joyce Carol Oates, and see how she wants it treated and publish it accordingly."

The matter is complicated by the fact that in August Dutton will publish Miss Oates's new novel, *You Must Remember This*, a story set in the 1950's about a 14-year-old girl who is in love with her uncle, a professional boxer. While it is not unprecedented for novels by the same author to be published in one year, publishers tend to think that one book a year—particularly in fiction—by an author is about as much as customers, reviewers and literary critics will bear.

"I'm quite stunned at this piece of news," Mr. Abrahams, who edited *You Must Remember This*, said. "I'm in an odd position since I'm her editor and I should know what she's doing. *You Must Remember This* is the most remarkable book she's ever written, and we're putting a tremendous amount of effort in it."

Ms. Gregory was equally bewildered. "I just can't understand it," she said. "She hasn't written under pseudonyms before."

Lives of the Twins, Miss Oates said, originated with a mystery detective novel she wrote a few years ago, *Mysteries of Winterthurn*.

"I became fascinated with the genre and thought I'd like to do something along those lines," she explained. "Last summer I wrote a psychological mystery, quite short, very experimental. I think of it almost as a prose movie. It moves very swiftly and it's very different from what I think of as a traditional novel."

Because it is unlike her usual writing, she did not show it to Mr. Abrahams or Ms. Gregory. Instead, she gave it to Rosalie Siegel, a literary agent and neighbor in Princeton. "I knew if Blanche submitted it to editors they might recognize it," she said. "I wanted a fresh reading; I wanted to escape from my own identity." They accepted the first offer, a $10,000 advance.

Several years ago Doris Lessing revealed that she had written two novels under the pseudonym Jane Somers to dramatize the difficulties faced by unknown writers. But Miss Oates said that was not her intention. "I didn't think of it as a trick," she said. "I just thought of it as something different."

Miss Oates, the author of nearly 40 books, including novels, short stories, poetry and essays, is distinguished not only for the quantity of her output but also for her wide range of literary genres and non-fiction subjects. One current subject is boxing. An article she wrote for *The New York Times Magazine* has been expanded into the book *On Boxing*, which Dolphin-Doubleday will publish next month. She and Dan Halpern are co-editors of an anthology, *The Poetics of Boxing*, that Henry Holt is scheduled to publish in 1988. And her account of the Mike Tyson-Trevor Berbick heavyweight fight in Las Vegas last November will appear in *Life* magazine in March.

Meanwhile, Miss Oates said she was sorry her effort to obtain a "fresh reading" from editors and critics was spoiled by the revelation that she was the author of *Lives of The Twins*. In a voice tinged with regret she said, "That's the last time I'll try to use a pseudonym."

A Heavyweight Looks at Boxing

George Vecsey/1987

From *The New York Times*, 4 March 1987. © 1987 *The New York Times* Co. Reprinted by permission.

Joyce Carol Oates does not like tennis "or any other game that is one-on-one." She attributes that lack of interest not to any possible lack of physical ability as to an absence of aggression.

As she discusses tennis briefly, she gives off a personal disinclination to corner another human being, to bash a forehand, to deliver a 6-0 drubbing to friend or stranger.

"I'm not aggressive," she said. "That's one reason I'm fascinated by boxing, that two people can climb in the ring and do that. I mean, I'm probably as horrified by boxing as you are. I'm also mystified by it."

As one of the very best novelists, she can relate to the monastic side of boxers, that makes them shut off human contact and expose themselves to pain.

"My husband sometimes says to me, 'If you keep writing like that, you'll make yourself sick,' " she said. "When I was little, I loved to read at night and my mother would say, 'You'll ruin your eyes.' "

As a feminist, she is fascinated by boxing's link to "male rage," and also by what her curiosity says about Joyce Carol Oates.

"This is the closest thing to an autobiography I'm likely to do," she said yesterday over her second breakfast and second interview of the young morning. Listening to a local scribbler work out his own problems with boxing is the kind of boxerlike punishment authors learn to absorb while escorting a new book into public.

The new book is titled *On Boxing*, published by Dolphin/Doubleday, with exquisite photographs by John Ranard. Ms. Oates is not looking for a knockout, the justification of boxing, because "as a novelist, I am not a propagandist," she said. "I shrink from it." Yet she delivers an artistic dancing-and-jabbing triumph worthy of a Sugar Ray Robinson.

She is perfect in describing the single-mindedness of a Rocky

Marciano, the bitterness of a Larry Holmes, the gentility of a Mike
Tyson, and the dreams of "the contenders," to whom the book is
dedicated.

There is a marvelous photograph of an anonymous thick-waisted
boxer with hairy shoulders and an advancing forehead, trying to
scowl like Sonny Liston, against a peeling wall. Ms. Oates would not
deny this "opponent," this "bum-of-the-month," his chance to spill
blood for his dream.

But that is where Ms. Oates and her breakfast companion differed.
He would push the button on boxing, just as he would push the
button on smoking in public, and a few other practices, if given the
chance.

"I don't want to sound like a sexist," she said, "but men often
think they know what is good for other people."

She thinks male aggression is a combination of hormones and
social conditioning, and she is fascinated by it. She writes about
being introduced to boxing by her father, and how, years later, she
returned to boxing during research about the 40's and 50's.

"I'm not a fan," she said, and she does not consider boxing a
sport.

Boxing is covered, however, as a sport. Her breakfast companion
came out for abolition of boxing after watching people cheer the
punches that led to the death of Duk Koo Kim in 1982. My position is
that society has the right to protect the health of its members,
sometimes even by banishing activities.

"I would not want to think about taking away their livelihood—
Mike Tyson without boxing," Ms. Oates said. "Should we abolish
lyric poetry because a number of lyric poets have a tendency toward
alcohol and suicide?"

One could argue that many drugs are illegal; that seat-belts are
mandatory; that child pornography and cock-fighting and slavery are
against the law. When will we get around to banning a "sport" in
which the goal is to deliver a minideath, a knockout?

"To be knocked out doesn't mean what it seems," Ms. Oates said.
"A boxer does not have to get up."

She traces the drive of boxers to the "partially justified anger" of
immigrants and the underclass. Talking about her upbringing in

Buffalo she added, "Since I don't come from the middle class, I can understand."

There is certainly honor in trying to fight one's way from the ghetto, but is that enough to make a writer tolerate boxing? Ms. Oates finds the celebrated articles of A. J. Liebling to be "relentlessly jokey, condescending, and occasionally racist."

It has long been my opinion that many writers in the past could not have written so casually, so prettily, about coal miners, deformed and unhealthy, as they did about practitioners of this "sport."

In a fine new book, *Sugar Ray Leonard and Other Noble Warriors*, published by McGraw-Hill, Sam Toperoff wrote: "If I could not justify boxing deaths or the exploitation of fighters, I could at least see boxing's comparative virtues. In the ring you see two men, unpackaged, damn near naked, in fact. The species itself, un-adorned. . . .

"The balance between mind and body in the 'advanced' societies has tipped heavily toward self-justifying mind, and the imbalance diminishes us terribly," Toperoff added. "Boxing, if it does nothing else, at least restores the blood to its place of importance."

Ms. Oates is also fascinated by the shedding of this basic fluid of life. Exposing herself to boxing, she found herself half in a dream, half in a nightmare, averting her face until her curious side made her turn back.

"What about auto racing?" she asks, recalling a gruesome half hour of television, a crash, an announcement that a driver, "the father of 11," had been taken to the hospital. She is sure the viewers "were only interested in the crashes."

Would she ban auto racing? She perks up. "I might start there," she said. She does not play tennis, but for the moment she delivers a verbal overhand smash. Point, Ms. Oates.

My Writing Is Full of Lives I Might Have Led

Jay Parini/1987

From *The Boston Globe Magazine*, 2 August 1987. © 1987 *The Boston Globe*. Reprinted by permission.

Joyce Carol Oates is one of those people who live in glass houses—quite literally. She and her husband, Ray Smith, bought their large contemporary house with shimmering glass walls in 1978, when they moved to Princeton, New Jersey. The house is set in woodlands several miles from Princeton University, where Oates teaches, and its distance from the campus seems partly calculated to prevent students from casually dropping in. "We loved the house when we first saw it," says Oates, in her frank, almost flutelike voice. Her husband, she says, is extremely taken up with the garden these days. Oates, Smith, and I circle the property, looking at Smith's newly fenced-in garden. The pond, which is visible from the living room, is surrounded by high trees that shade its somewhat murky depths. As we climb back to the house, the thick woods echo with the song of an especially vibrant wood thrush. "That's the loveliest of all bird calls, I think," Oates says.

One steps into the living room but does not leave nature behind. With its floor-to-ceiling glass walls, the house seems not so much a shelter from the green world outside but a window into it. A white baby grand piano sits in one corner, a place where Oates often retreats when she's tired of writing. There are Oriental rugs on the hardwood floors, but the furniture is generally as contemporary as the house, which is built around an atrium in the Mediterranean style. The house seems an appropriately symbolic residence for a writer; in fact, Oates' novels, stories, poems, and plays might be thought of as windows to her soul. Though she is not an explicitly autobiographical writer, it's not hard to see where much of her material comes from. "My writing is full of lives I might have led," she says. "A writer imagines what could have happened, not what really happened."

We go into Oates' study to talk. Set off on its own, in a far wing of

152

the house, the room is full of memorabilia: clippings from *The New York Times* about her recent book on boxing, various editions of her many books, photos. There is a comfortable couch, a coffee table covered with books, and a long desk that supports a pile of manuscripts-in-progress as well as Oates' relatively new computer. The computer, she says, has changed the way she works: Now she writes more slowly, making more corrections and more changes. She also looks forward to revision. Just in case the computer should break down, an old-fashioned typewriter sits nearby. A sad little anachronism, it looks as if it saw a lot of action in its salad days.

"I make endless notes before I begin writing a novel," Oates explains, picking up a large pile of jottings. "I always take notes when I travel." She appears to have scratched out odd scenes—bits of dialogue or description—for her current work-in-progress in the margins of a magazine, on the back of a theater program, on hotel stationery, or on miscellaneous scraps of paper. One rapidly gets the sense that Joyce Carol Oates never takes a minute off.

On a bulletin board just to the left of her computer screen there is a time chart with characters' names placed on a grid. "I like to know what will happen when and to whom," she says. She usually works with charts similar to this one, especially when the novel has a historical angle. When she was writing *The Crosswicks Horror*, which is set in Princeton in 1906, she put a map of the town on the wall, too. That novel, which she wrote a few years ago and is about to be revised, will be published in 1988. She is looking forward to revising: "Writing the first draft is the hard part, when you're actually trying to think of what happens next," Oates says. "That's quite painful. But the rest is fun."

Oates' new novel, *You Must Remember This*, will be published this month by Dutton. Her editor there, William Abrahams, says he thinks it's her best book yet. Dutton will print 50,000 copies, which Oates herself finds "a little scary," wondering if there are "so many readers out there." She, too, thinks the book is one of her best. "It's one of the most personal of my novels," she says. "It's set in the 1950s, but I don't think of it as an historical novel. I grew up in the '50s. It's all very real to me, though I did have to look up some things about bomb shelters."

She shows me a postcard from that outwardly placid decade which features a man in a small-town setting who is hard at work digging his bomb shelter. The man might well be Lyle Stevick, the earnest father of Enid, the new novel's late-adolescent heroine. The book's stark, realistic prose is quintessential Oates, a return to the muscularity and vividness of her earliest stories and novels. In one of the book's most poignant scenes, Lyle goes to borrow money from his brother, Felix (who happens to be sleeping with Enid):

" 'Felix, it's this: I'm in a quandary and I need money and I'd like to borrow it from you and I don't know when I'll be able to repay it.' The terrible words came out in a rush, Lyle's face burned. Seeing that Felix's expression hardly changed, he went on speaking quickly, gesturing with his pipe, the pent-up words tumbling about them. He needed $4,300 for the purpose of constructing an underground bomb shelter with at least four feet of earth between the roof of the shelter and the air as the Civil Defense people were now advocating, the latest disclosures were that an ordinary shelter in an ordinary basement would be all but useless given a saturation attack by the enemy."

You Must Remember This is set in a town similar to the one in which Oates grew up. "It takes place in a fictitious city, Port Oriskany," says Oates, "an amalgam of two cities in upstate New York—Buffalo, the first large city of my experience, and Lockport, the city of my birth, my paternal grandmother's home, suffused forever for me with the extravagant dreams of early adolescence." Oates remembers that "while writing the novel I had a map of Port Oriskany taped to my wall so that, dreamy as all novelists are, when not in the throes of acute anxiety or the fabled and so-often-elusive white heat of composition, I could simply stare at it." She describes the novel's heroine, Enid Stevick, as a character very like herself. "The novel's primary excitement for me," she says, "was its evocation of that now remote decade, 1946 to 1956."

With *You Must Remember This* Oates has once again written a novel that probes our deepest fears and foolish hopes in what W. H. Auden identified as the "age of anxiety." The novel appears to have been written with a strange urgency, and—as the best novels always do—it generates an aura, a sense of reality, all its own. *You Must Remember This* is vintage Oates, a novel written by an important writer at the height of her powers.

Oates, at 49, is tall and sylphlike, with a peculiar beauty that's hard to describe. Her dark hair is full of natural ringlets that seem to defy taming. "She is not photogenic," says Robert Phillips, a close friend. "No photo has ever done justice to her appearance, which conveys grace and high intelligence." She is also notoriously shy, avoiding publicity when she can (this is perhaps why she has put several miles between herself and the Princeton campus). "I'm not a public person like Gore Vidal or Norman Mailer," she acknowledges. "I just live here quietly and write every day and teach my classes at Princeton." She speaks of herself with characteristic modesty: "I hardly see myself as being unusual. I take my writing seriously, but I don't take myself seriously. That is, I don't feel pontifical or dogmatic. Writing is an absolutely fascinating activity, an immersion in drama, language, and vision."

Immersion is certainly the word for Joyce Carol Oates. Few writers have put more time into the actual process of writing. *You Must Remember This* is her 18th novel. She has also written 14 books of short stories, several plays, half a dozen critical books, several collections of poetry, and a vast quantity of journalism. "I suspect that Joyce never sleeps," says her Princeton colleague A. Walton Litz. "She's a phenomenon."

Searching for comparisons with earlier writers, one might think of Balzac—and Oates agrees. "I have a laughably Balzacian ambition to get the whole world into a book," she told Walter Clemons when he interviewed her for a *Newsweek* cover story in 1972. Expanding on this, she says, "A writer's job, ideally, is to act as the conscience of his race. People frequently misunderstand serious art because it is often violent and unattractive. I wish the world were a prettier place, but I wouldn't be honest as a writer if I ignored the actual conditions around me."

Balzac, in his series of novels, *The Human Comedy*, hoped to portray every aspect of contemporary French culture, from the working class to the bourgeoisie and aristocracy. Oates, in near emulation, has written with the same high ambition. Her early novels and stories were often set in the upstate New York landscape of her childhood, depicting lower-middle-class life in those windswept towns not far from Buffalo, places where, as Oates says, "no one expects to leave home." In *Expensive People* (1968), she wrote about the wealthy

suburban class that became the mainstay of John Cheever's fiction.
In *them* (the *t* is never capitalized), which was published in 1969 and
won the National Book Award in 1970, Oates portrays Detroit
working-class life against the background of riots that turned that city
into a flaming caldron. *Do with Me What You Will* (1973) is a portrait
of the legal profession in America, while *The Assassins* (1975) takes
for its subject the political world of Washington, a theme she returned
to in 1981 with *Angel of Light*, an Elizabethan revenge tragedy in
modern dress. *Son of the Morning* (1978) probes the seamy
underside of evangelical Protestantism in the tradition of *Elmer
Gantry*, while *Unholy Loves* (1979) takes a wry look at life on an
American college faculty. Again and again, Oates points the laser
beam of her art at a wide range of targets, often with startling
accuracy.

In 1980, she published her most commercially successful novel,
Bellefleur, which examines generations of the wealthy Bellefleur
family during the early years of the 19th century. It is a mock Gothic,
a huge, multilayered novel that prompted critic Marvin Mudrick to call
Oates "the fourth Bronte sister." This was followed by a popular
series of pseudo-Gothic, romance, and mystery novels that parody
their respective genres with great intelligence and wit. The culminat-
ing volume in this series is the forthcoming Princeton novel, *The
Crosswicks Horror*, which has Woodrow Wilson as a central
character. "I like to call these novels 'parodistic,' " says Oates.
"They're not exactly parodies, because they take the forms they
imitate quite seriously."

What do the critics make of Joyce Carol Oates? Opinions seem to
vary wildly. "Oates may be the finest American novelist, man or
woman, since Faulkner," writes Robert H. Fossum, who has been
echoed by dozens of other critics. J. A. Avant calls Oates "one of
America's best writers of short stories," and A. P. Klauser describes
The Assassins as "a parable of our times." Out in what Gore Vidal
calls "Bookchat Land," there is a great deal of hype. But there is also
a great deal of venom. It is unseemly to write so many books so
quickly, and for them to be so good. *Newsweek* called *them* "a
charnel house of Gothic paraphernalia: blood, fire, insanity, anarchy,
lust, corruption, death by bullets, death by cancer, death by plane
crash, death by stabbing, beatings, crime, riot, and even unhap-

piness." Michael Wood, writing in *The New York Times Book Review*, said that Oates' fiction was "self-indulgent, a refusal by the writer to know what she knows." In a fairly typical move, *Time* recently called her "the somewhat too prodigious Joyce Carol Oates," suggesting that she ought to "steady her grip" on her writing.

In response to the accusation of overproduction, Oates heaves a sigh of impatience. "It's really insignificant," she says. "What is ultimately important is a writer's strongest books." As to the omnipresent charge that her work features too much violence, she says, "Given the number of pages I've written, and then the 'violent' incidents dispersed throughout them, I rather doubt that I am a violent writer in any meaningful sense of that word." As if to further explain the violent acts that often explain her characters' motivation, she says, "My grandfather was murdered, and I suppose that act of violence has always haunted me. It's always there, at the back of my mind."

Born in 1938, Oates grew up outside Lockport on a farm with her maternal grandparents. Her parents, Frederic and Carolina Oates, are kindly, straightforward people who recognized their daughter's abilities at an early age. "She was always so hard-working" says her mother, "a perfectionist at everything. Once she was asked to memorize some Bible verses for a church contest. The child who could memorize the most verses would win a free week at summer camp. Joyce worked so hard at that. She could recite reams of verses, and, of course, she won the week at camp." Her father, a tool-and-die designer by trade, adds, "We never really thought she'd be *this* successful. It all started when she was in college and won that fiction contest at *Mademoiselle*. Everything just took off from there."

The affection between Mr. and Mrs. Oates and their famous daughter is certainly mutual; like the heroine of her first novel, *With Shuddering Fall* (1964), Oates has made peace with her background. "I'm extremely close to my parents," she notes. Her father, she says with pride, recently retired and enrolled in a course at a university in Buffalo. "He and my mother are both fond of books. They love to read." Her parents were especially pleased this past spring when their daughter was given the key to the city of Lockport. "My mother and I were both given keys to the city," Oates explains, with mild embarrassment.

Oates attended Syracuse University on a New York State Regents Scholarship and graduated in 1960 at the top of her class, Phi Beta Kappa, with a degree in English. Her first break, as her father notes, came in 1959, in her junior year, when a story called "In the Old World" won a prize from *Mademoiselle*, though Oates was not yet committed to writing. She went off to the University of Wisconsin on a fellowship, where she got a master's degree in English and met Ray Smith, whom she married the same year. After a brief start on her doctorate at Rice University in Texas, she abandoned graduate school and professional criticism for fiction, publishing her first book of stories, *By the North Gate*, in 1963. But she has never stopped teaching. She likes teaching, she says, and wouldn't want to give it up. She teaches only in the afternoons, usually two afternoons a week. "It lends a balance to my day, creates a rhythm that's good for working."

During the tempestuous years of the late '60s, she was teaching at the University of Detroit—an exciting time to be in that particular city. Her novel *them* reflects all the terror and confusion of that troubled decade: "In *them*," writes Ellen G. Friedman, who has done a full-length study of Oates' fiction, "Oates creates a violent, indeed apocalyptic world, one that seems at times in the final stages of disintegration, punctuated by terrible cataclysms, and bursting with malevolent passions." Late in the '60s, Oates and Smith moved across the border to Canada, lured by an offer from the University of Windsor. In retreat from her Detroit period, Oates settled down to some hard work, publishing no fewer than 27 books in a decade.

With their move to Princeton nine years ago, Oates and Smith seem to have settled down once and for all. "It was like coming home," says Oates, "since Princeton isn't really very far from where I grew up." Oates is writer-in-residence at Princeton University, with a half-time teaching load, and Smith is editor of *The Ontario Review*, a literary quarterly that he and Oates cofounded when they were teaching at Windsor. They brought the magazine with them to Princeton. Smith also runs The Ontario Review Press, which publishes books of poetry and fiction, often by little-known or beginning writers. "Ray is an extremely hard worker," says Oates. "We both start each day at about 7:30 or 8, right after breakfast, and we're often still working at midnight."

Oates has recently been in the headlines for a book she wrote under the pseudonym of Rosamond Smith that will be published next winter. (The pseudonym is obviously a feminization of her husband's name.) "It isn't my usual sort of novel," explains Oates. "It's a mystery novel, what I like to think of as a 'concept' novel, not a 'real' novel. A real novel is many-layered, complex, with lots of different characters and subplots, and the language is terribly important. But a concept novel is more like a movie scenario, with lots of dialogue." She wrote the mystery novel, called *Lives of the Twins*, very quickly, and because it was so different from her previous work, she didn't want to publish it under her own name. So she and her neighbor, Rosalie Siegel, who happens to be a literary agent, concocted a plan. "It was a lot of fun, at first," Oates confesses. "We liked having this little secret." Submitting the novel to an editor at Simon & Schuster, Nancy Nicholas, Siegel pretended that Rosamond Smith was a young first-novelist with no reputation. Nicholas liked *Lives of the Twins* and accepted it, paying an advance of $10,000. All would have gone as planned had not a friend of Oates leaked the news to the press. "I wish he hadn't done that," says Oates. "I wanted to escape my identity, and this was a way to do that."

This little caper upset everyone, of course: Nancy Nicholas, who had been duped, as well as Oates' long-time agent, Blanche Gregory, and her devoted editor at Dutton, William Abrahams, who says he was "quite stunned by the news." He was especially concerned because of the upcoming publication of *You Must Remember This*. Blanche Gregory says, "I just couldn't understand it. She's never written under pseudonyms before." Oates is troubled to have upset close friends and supporters. "I didn't think of it as a trick," she says. "I just thought of it as something different." She adds, "That's the last time I'll try to use a pseudonym."

Oates has also been in the news with her recent book on boxing. Indeed, she has always had an interest in the sport, but when she began to write *You Must Remember This*, which features an amateur boxer, Felix Stevick, she started to look closely at it. "Boxing is an American sport—a 'so-called sport' to many—in which images of incalculable beauty and violence, desperation and ingenuity, are routinely entwined," she says. "The sport evokes the most extreme reactions—loathing, revulsion, righteous indignation, a fierce and often inexplicable loyalty." She loves to sit back and reminisce about her favorite fighters of the past: Sugar Ray Robinson, Rocky Marciano, Archie Moore, Jersey Joe Walcott, and Carmen Basilio. She wrote an article on boxing for *The New York Times Magazine* that was recently expanded into a small book, *On Boxing*, published by Dolphin-Doubleday. And soon Holt will publish *The Poetics of Boxing*, an anthology she coedited with a friend, the poet Daniel Halpern. Last spring, an article with references to the Mike Tyson-Trevor Berbick heavyweight fight appeared in *Life*.

How can one account for this phenomenon called Joyce Carol Oates? No one really knows. "She's hard to place as a writer," says Robert Cowley, a senior editor at Holt. "Because she writes so much, many readers and critics don't take her as seriously as they should. She's a very serious writer, in fact." In *Bright Book of Life*, his well-known study of contemporary fiction, Alfred Kazin puts a finger on something essential about Oates, saying that her "characters move through a world that seems to be wholly physical and even full of global eruption. . . . They touch us by frightening us, like disembodied souls calling to us from the other world. They live through terrifying events but cannot understand them. This is what makes Oates a new element in our fiction, involuntarily disturbing."

Oates is like a medium, gazing into the crystal ball of her computer screen, calling up lives and worlds that eerily reflect and illumine our own. Her work is oddly unprocessed; it's as if she refuses to translate her vision for us, to mediate between us and the world of her imagination. Again, the glass-house metaphor seems appropriate. We, as readers, are allowed to look directly into the interior regions of her soul. The glass is never clouded, though it may be tinted. What we see may be, as Kazin says, "involuntarily disturbing," but so be it.

Oates understands what she is doing, of course. Talking to her, one becomes aware that she is a highly self-conscious artist, perfectly aware of what she is doing or not doing. And she knows exactly how she differs from those who are not artists. "Every person dreams," she says, "and every dreamer is a kind of artist. The formal artist is one who arranges his dreams into a shape that can be experienced by other people. There is no guarantee that art will be understood, not even by the artist; it is not meant to be understood but to be experienced."

Making Readers Want Novels Is Writer's Hardest Job

Michele Weldon/1987

From *The Dallas Times Herald*, 12 November 1987, F3-4. ©
1987 *The Dallas Times Herald*. Reprinted by permission.

The rain pounds the sidewalk in slams and thuds. Students hurry into
Hyer Hall, wearing denim jackets that hang like damp blankets on
their shoulders. Up the stairs slick from rain-soaked shoes, almost 80
Southern Methodist University freshmen in Martha Satz's Monday 9
a.m. honors English class wait in Room 200 for Joyce Carol Oates.

It is a heady day, fit for a novelist.

The renowned author of nearly 40 books—including novels, essays
and poetry—slips into the room and takes a seat in the front row,
looking frightened and shy, with all the command of a check-out
clerk in a small-town grocery. She is alarmingly thin, her black pants
hanging loosely, a flesh-colored T-shirt and black cardigan embracing
her narrow frame. Her auburn hair is permed with awkward curls and
her lips are brightened with a mulberry lipstick that matches the
frames of her glasses. Then there are her eyes. Her eyes are wide and
racing, giving her the appearance of a doe trapped in fear.

The 49-year-old professor of creative writing at Princeton University and former professor at University of Detroit and the University of
Windsor in Ontario steps to the podium after a glowing introduction
from Satz. In Dallas for a reading of some of her work Sunday at the
SMU Literary Festival, and for this morning's class, Oates is apologetic and says she thought she was addressing a writing class, so she
asks the students for questions.

"I'm sort of amazed at all these people," she says as she looks
away from the crowd. But then the stumbling shyness is gone, falling
like a curtain when she talks about her work. Oates is forthright and
witty, with all the stamina and strength of a featherweight champion
in the ring with an unprepared opponent.

"The last thing anybody really wants is another novel," she says,
her hands punctuating each sentence. "Nobody is knocking on your

door for another poem or another novel. . . . You're doing something very gratuitous that nobody really wants, so the challenge is to make them want it."

Apparently enough people have wanted what Oates has churned from her typewriter, because the winner of the National Book Award is constantly at work. Having finished her most recent novel, *You Must Remember This*, Oates is at work on a collection of essays called *Being a Woman Writer* and a screenplay. The title of her book of essays is somewhat tongue-in-cheek: "I don't think of myself as a woman writer," Oates tells the class. "Just a writer, an American writer."

Oates lifts the top of the podium and peers inside it, as if her curiosity is so uncontrollable she needs to scrutinize everything in her immediate radius. She responds to another question, this one about success. "I'm not a best seller. If I make a lot of money, it's almost by accident. The word success I would never use, failure is more the common lot of humanity."

Later, tucked in a small windowless office with bare metal book-shelves and frameless posters taped to the wall, Oates is even more relaxed and talks more personally about her life.

Born in Lockport, N.Y., 50 years ago next June, Oates says she is not from a wealthy family, but not underprivileged, either. "Our family has had problems, economic, things like that," she says quietly in a tone that is decidedly Midwestern. She says she has an autistic sister 18 years younger than she and a brother who is a draftsman in upstate New York.

"I am very close to my parents," Oates says. Her 72-year-old father, Frederick Oates, she says, was forced to quit school in the eighth grade and go to work. Her 71-year-old mother, Carolina, was given away when she was a baby because her father was murdered and her mother was too poor to raise her.

"I know they've had a hard life. People today are more spoiled. It's one of the themes of my writing," Oates says. "I have never had problems like my mother and father, but now they have this happy life."

Oates graduated from Syracuse University in 1960, and in 1961 received her master's degree from the University of Wisconsin. It was there she met her husband of 25 years, Raymond Smith, a former professor who's now editor and publisher of *The Ontario Review.*

This is her first trip to Dallas and she wants to talk about her impressions. "The thing about Dallas that interests me, haunts me, is this landscape of extraordinary buildings: the green neon, the rocket building, the needle building." Her voice falters and she sounds almost hurt. "Then you learn later they are foreclosed and empty. It is the dominant image to me."

Outside of Dallas, Oates says, she is recognized many places she goes but she is not harassed by fans. She has, however, been asked to sign napkins in restaurants. But that is rare. "People who read books tend to be more restrained." She laughs. "I'm not like Madonna."

The conversation goes back to her parents.

"We all feel a little sad that life moves on," Oates says. "People you love are going to be dying. The world gets more lonely. I guess that's what I think about." Then she smiles. "If I was still looking for a husband, I'd be a little disturbed at this point."

Joyce Carol Oates Keeps Punching

Robert Compton/1987

From *The Dallas Morning News*, 17 November 1987, 5C. ©
1987 *The Dallas Morning News*. Reprinted by permission.

"I'm taller than Sylvester Stallone," revealed wispy, 5-foot, 8-inch
Joyce Carol Oates.

"I look down on him," the literary heavyweight continued,
perfectly enunciating a verbal *double entendre* aimed at the movies'
Rocky/Rambo. If Stallone (she pronounces it "Stah-yone") appears
to be taller than his female film co-stars, it may be that he wears
elevator shoes, she guessed.

Oates, while opening Southern Methodist University's 13th annual
Literary Festival last week, remarked on the "Italian Stallion" as an
aside to the readings she was about to do for an audience of some
200 in McFarlin Auditorium. In a chatty introduction to a reading
from her non-fiction philosophical essay, *On Boxing*, Oates said she
met Stallone last March in Las Vegas, where she was reporting for
Life magazine on the Mike Tyson-Leroy Holmes heavyweight fight.

Tyson was the subject of the *Life* article. "Fortunately, he won,"
remarked the author. That story assignment from *Life* resulted from
an earlier, philosophical Oates essay on the sport of boxing for *The
New York Times*. And that essay—extended somewhat—became her
book, *On Boxing*, which was published earlier this year.

"I've been fascinated with boxing for a long time," said Oates,
whose recent novel *You Must Remember This* also contains allusions
to the sport. Producing two books in less than a year is not unusual
for the author, who has been applauded by critics each time she
ventures into another literary genre. And few genres have escaped
her attention. She is a poet, a novelist, an essayist, a critic, a writer of
short stories. Her credits would fill a small book.

At SMU, she chose to read some short poems, including some
about boxing ("Undefeated Heavyweight, 20 Years Old: One" and
"Undefeated Heavyweight, 20 Years Old: Two"); another about a
middle-aged North Carolina waitress who cherishes her memory of

serving a young Elvis Presley ("Waiting on Elvis, 1956"); yet another
on the smells of northern New Jersey, where she lives ("Night
Driving, 1987"). And one on leeches—"the subject is so repulsive I
can't name it," she shuddered. Its title: "Your Blood in a Little Puddle
on the Ground."

Oates described her "Waiting on Elvis" as a "found" poem. "My
husband and I love to travel," she said. "We like to go by car, to see
the country. We stopped at a cafe in a city in North Carolina and saw
all these photographs of Elvis. The waitress there had waited on Elvis
many years ago, an Elvis who looked very young in the pictures. The
older Elvis was bloated with his own fame. America has a strange
fascination with fame, something strange and almost allegorical."

"Night Driving" was "found" in a more personal sense, the author
explained, while driving home from Manhattan, "sometimes with rain
coming down in sheets, my husband sleeping beside me, and the
factory smells of northern New Jersey all about—really awful—but
somehow comforting, sort of beautiful, because it's familiar, it's home.
We find beauty and solace sometimes in something we shouldn't."

The writer's fascination with boxing was evident in her readings
and commentaries. In that sport, she finds, if not beauty, high
drama—"tragic theater." In particular, she talked about Tyson, who,
like many recent ring champions, is black and from the streets.
"Tyson said all his boyhood friends are dead or in prison. Boxing was
redemptive for him.

"For the most part, boxers belong to the disenfranchised of our
society, to impoverished ghetto neighborhoods. This is work to them,
and the appearance of anger is not real. It is a sort of symbolic anger.
Larry Holmes once said, 'You ever been black? I was black once—
when I was poor.' "

There is, the author maintained, a certain relationship between
writing and boxing. "The training goes on and on. There is one
important difference—a boxer's career ends at an early age; writers
can go on into their 90s."

At the close of her readings, Oates invited questions from the
audience. After an initial hesitation, the queries began.

What does she read? "The great poets, modern poets" and classic
novelists such as Thomas Hardy, D.H. Lawrence. "Most of all, (19th-
century American poet) Emily Dickinson. "She is inexhaustible."

When did she first publish? "I was in high school. In college I entered writing contests. I tell my students (in creative writing at Princeton University) they should enter writing contests as often as possible. Participation is important."

What are her work habits? "In the white heat of composition, I write 10 hours a day. That isn't usual. I like to work in the morning. The first six weeks of a novel are the hardest for me. It's so depressing, so demoralizing to know that you're failing. You can't write the first line of a novel until you write the last line.

"Getting the first draft finished is like pushing a peanut with your nose across a very dirty floor."

A Day in the Life
Rita D. Jacobs/1987

From *T.W.A. Ambassador*, December 1987, 52-53, 65-67. ©
1987 T.W.A. Ambassador. Reprinted by permission.

The house is nestled into a wooded landscape several miles from
Princeton University, where Joyce Carol Oates teaches. Constructed
around an atrium, the one-story building is lined with glass walls, and
at every turn the eye lights on a lush and wild natural scene outside.
Inside, serenity and order reign. The long living room is balanced at
one end by a white baby grand piano and at the other by a large
highly polished dining table. In between, a small sofa and comfortable chairs are clustered for conversation around a table. On an
upholstered side chair a calico cat stretches luxuriously as another, fat
and white with a surprising raccoon-striped tail, saunters by. Oates,
elegantly lean and tall, dressed in a simple skirt and a blouse that her
mother made for her, bends over to stroke the calico.

It is afternoon. Mornings are reserved for writing, not visitors. "I
can't imagine why anyone would want to watch me write, anyway,"
Oates says when I call to make arrangements for my visit, "there's
nothing to see." An early riser, Oates is at her desk by 8:00 or 8:30
each day and writes until about one. Sometimes she spends even
longer periods at her desk. "When I'm really involved or getting
towards the end of a novel, I can write for up to ten hours a day. At
those times, it's as though I'm writing a letter to someone I'm desperately in love with."

Given both her productivity—18 novels, 13 collections of short
stories, 8 books of poetry, 5 books of criticism, 2 collections of plays,
and numerous articles—and her enthusiastic audience, I would say
that Joyce Carol Oates has had an enormously successful love affair
with literature. As early as 1970, when she was only 32, she won the
National Book Award for 1969 for her novel *them*, and in 1972,
Newsweek featured her in a cover story, calling her "the most significant novelist to have emerged in the United States in the last
decade."

We walk down a corridor strewn with Oriental rugs past a closed door behind which I hear the sound of someone on the phone. "That's Ray. He's in his study working." Raymond Smith, her husband of 26 years, runs The Ontario Review Press and is editor of *The Ontario Review*, a small, prestigious literary magazine they co-founded in 1974. Oates and Smith met at a faculty tea when they were graduate students at the University of Wisconsin; three weeks later they were married.

Her study at the end of the hall is plainly furnished. The writing desk sits in front of a large window that looks out on a confusion of grass and trees. The only signs of civilization are two white wrought-iron lawn chairs that sit side by side in a small clearing as though they await occupants. The desk is clean except for a Smith Corona portable typewriter topped by a pile of manuscript pages, single-spaced and marked over with pen and pencil scrawls of revision. Oates points to the pages. "That's a new novel I'm working on," she says softly. "It's odd, the computer is in the shop being repaired and I was sure I'd miss it terribly, but now that I'm back to the typewriter I find that I'm perfectly happy with it."

The bulletin board on the wall next to the desk is haphazardly decorated with a newspaper ad for her latest novel, *You Must Remember This*, and a glowing *New York Times* review of the book. Beneath these clippings are two startlingly colored reproductions of Georgia O'Keeffe's flower paintings, one flush with hot pink petals, the other a brilliant red poppy.

In a pin-neat house filled with exquisite art, Oriental rugs, and yards of bookshelves, the only disarray seems to appear on bulletin boards. In the kitchen a large board is filled with pictures of places she's visited—there's a lovely photo that Ray took of her on the beach in California, a small figure confronting the Pacific's huge waves—and many of her friends and her parents, who still live in Millersport, New York, the five-house town where Oates was born.

A tall, bespectacled, and rather handsome man appears in the doorway of the kitchen. "Would you like something to drink?" asks Ray. He brings our soft drinks into what was once a garage and has now been renovated into a cozy sitting room lined with books and warmed by a free-standing white fireplace. As we talk about literary politics, the New York Mets, boxing, travel, and the couple's favorite

jogging paths, Ray's eyes often focus with great affection and attention on Joyce. That decision made after three weeks of courtship
twenty-six years ago appears to have been the right one for both of
them.

Oates's afternoon schedule is usually determined by her teaching
duties and the academic demands of meetings and conferences. This
afternoon, though, she's on her way to New York to give a reading at
an Upper West Side bookstore.

At six o'clock, we arrive in the city. Marvin Gutin, an avid boxing
fan and co-owner of Marvin Gardens restaurant on Upper Broadway
in Manhattan, has invited Oates to dinner. He had written her a fan
letter about On Boxing and was excited and nervous about meeting
her. Even before we were seated, he began his compliments. "Your
book on boxing was a marvel, you really made me think about the
reasons I love the sport."

Oates is pleased. She's gotten a lot of raves for this book that has
reached people who have never read any of her other work, even
though she jokes about the breadth of her topics and the scope of her
audience: "There was one month that I had articles in both Philo-
logical Quarterly and Playboy." Her productivity has raised critics'
eyebrows and readers' curiosity; this book marked a change. "I'm so
thrilled by the boxing book," she says. "Now at least people are
eager to talk to me about the content of a book. It's so much more
interesting than having to respond to the question 'How do you do
it?' "

As she eagerly talks boxing with Gutin, I struggle to keep up. These
two aficionados rattle off names and details of remembered bouts like
old fight managers. I am amazed by the scope of her knowledge.
"My father's best friend was a boxer," she tells us, "and they used to
spar together. Boxing was part of my childhood—it was an important
part of that working-class background. And for me it raised all kinds
of questions about masculinity. What does it mean to be a man? The
questions are unanswerable but provocative. I was fascinated by
boxing."

The fascination has continued. She knows the history of the sport,
the technical details, the managers, and the fighters (her particular
current favorite is Mike Tyson). This knowledge, combined with her
special brand of warmth—she does not suffer fools gladly, but when

engaged listens with a reserved but avid absorption—move Gutin to admit that her book enabled him to look at the darker side of himself, to confess with some embarrassment his eagerness to see a fighter he didn't like be hit.

By now it's close to eight o'clock and she's due to read from *You Must Remember This*. We walk the two blocks to Columbus Avenue where Endicott Booksellers, an old-fashioned, wood-paneled, and book-lined store, is located. Endicott is crowded, filled with people who've come to hear her read. At the door a young man approaches her, hand outstretched. He identifies himself as an admirer, a writer, and a boxer.

One of the amazing things about Oates is that she never seems hurried. She engages the young man in a conversation that might have gone on for a long time if Encarnita Quinlan, Endicott's owner, hadn't rushed up looking harried and apologetic. "The air conditioning's gone out. We're trying to have it repaired, but I don't know how long it will take. It may be necessary to cut the reading short." Oates, unflustered, takes the news in stride and says she's ready to try for the half hour or 45 minutes as planned.

In the back of the store a small table is set up for the reader. The crowd is so large that people are sitting on the floor as well as on chairs, and some are standing patiently waiting for Oates to begin. The crowd is hushed and expectant as she makes her way to the table.

Somewhat self-effacing and shy in one-on-one encounters, Oates lights up in front of the crowd. Immediately in command, she jokes about the heat. Jean Rawitt, director of marketing at Dutton, her publisher, looks over at me and smiles. Joyce has this under control.

She begins by giving the audience a glimpse of the writer's struggle to create with a surprising story about a period in her life when she encountered a writing block. "I had all these ideas for writing poetry and somehow nothing coalesced for three weeks. That's a long period of time if you're sitting there thinking and writing and not keeping anything. After all those days and hours, all I had was this one poem. I thought it was the beginning of a poetry phase but it was the only one I wrote, so actually it was the end of the phase. I realized it was really the beginning of the novel that became *You Must Remember This*."

The portion she reads revolves around a boxing match. Enid
Stevick, the young heroine, is taken by her father to see her Uncle
Felix fight. "To research the novel I watched hours of boxing films
dating back to 1909. I saw in these a kind of male history of America,
so I took a break from the novel and wrote *On Boxing*, which
became a meditation on masculinity seen from the outside. I had
thought I'd be more critical of boxing and of that kind of exaggerated
masculinity, but I wasn't." She pauses, and a smile plays about her
mouth as she surveys her audience. "I don't mean all men are judged
by these standards. Not at all, certainly not where I come from, not in
Princeton. There a man is judged by the length of his bibliography."

She reads the selection and then asks for questions. Clearly there
are those in the audience who are uncomfortable with Oates's passion for boxing. For most of her writing life, Oates has had to
confront the questions that arise because of the contrast between her
calm, demure appearance and the harsh and passionate reality of her
work. A critic once said that "if you met her at a literary party and
failed to catch her name, it might be hard to imagine her reading,
much less writing, the unflinching fiction of Joyce Carol Oates."

But she is certainly unflinching as she explains the lure, the beauty,
of boxing. She is intense, and behind her glasses her huge dark eyes
fulfill an early description: they do indeed seem to be "burning in a
dove's face." She talks about discovering a bare and essential truth.
"It is amazing in the midst of the nonsense and vulgarity of Las Vegas
to find a performer like Mike Tyson. In the very center of something
so meretricious, you can find this very real event—well that fascinates
me. It's not a metaphor for anything—it is something itself."

After the reading, a long line of people wait for her to autograph
just-bought copies of the new book or earlier works they've brought
along. She listens attentively to each of them, signing the dedications
they ask for. A high school English teacher brings a copy of a text-
book Oates edited; an older man wants her to sign the new novel for
his wife for a homecoming present. Her fans are devoted; sometimes
they even bring poems dedicated to her or portraits they've painted
of her.

Toward the end of this line stands a young woman with a very pale
face, long black hair, and an outfit featuring her bare midriff. She's
dressed for a downtown club and is oddly out of place in a crowd of

students, young professionals, and middle-aged intellectuals. But Tama Janowitz's face is certainly recognizable from the publicity that surrounded the publication of her stories, *Slaves of New York*. Oates looks up and smiles, "Tama, how good to see you." They hug and talk for a while about Janowitz's new writing project before Oates goes on to sign the rest of the books.

The day has been filled with writing, new people, public events, and intense conversations, yet at the end of it Oates is calm and gracious. When Dutton's hired limousine arrives to take her back to Princeton, she actually thanks *me* for a lovely day. It's only 9:30 PM, and as I stroll down Columbus Avenue I imagine that she's probably returning home to a cup of herbal tea and perhaps a few hours of writing before she retires.

Author Oates Tells Where She's Been, Where She's Going

David Germain/1988

From *The Union Sun & Journal*, 24 March 1988, 16. © 1988 *Lockport Union Sun & Journal*. Reprinted by permission.

Modest and unassuming, Joyce Carol Oates has moved like a quietly humming, well-tuned all-terrain vehicle over the rocky hills and swampy ravines of American literature.

She's done it all, from award-winning short stories and novels to masterful poetry and drama to insightful sports commentary. And she's done it without the self-aggrandizement of the '80s writer, the fanfare that announces the publication of one of the literati's latest books. Fanfare would cut into her writing time, which she values above all else. So she and her husband, editor and critic Raymond Smith, keep their noses in their books, far from the madding crowd, away from the hoopla and hype of much of the literary establishment.

Oates, who grew up just south of Lockport, lets her writing do the talking. She's cast her voice from academic halls to the boxing ring to the Kremlin.

Soviet leader Mikhail Gorbachev was impressed by the political overtones in Oates' novel *Angel of Light*; Gorbachev and his wife told her so at a meeting with some of America's top artists and scientists during the Communist chief's visit here last December.

Sports announcers have turned to Oates for ringside commentary, recognizing her expertise as an observer of boxing, and an observer of the observers of boxing. Her interest has brought her into the inner circle of heavyweight champion Mike Tyson and other boxers. She's never taken a punch in the ring, yet her novel *You Must Remember This* and her book-length essay *On Boxing* put the glove to readers' faces as vividly as a 15-round bloodbath on HBO.

Through it all, Oates remains aloof, aware of the spotlight turned on her, but looking up in mild surprise only for a quick glimpse of its dazzle before lowering her eyes again to her writing.

Oates looked up long enough Wednesday for a telephone interview with the Union-Sun & Journal from her
home in Princeton, N.J.

She was pleased that her home town honored her this
month with a festival at the Kenan Center focusing on her
work. That festival, which features artworks, classes and
screenings of films based on her writing, ends this week-
end.

Oates also had fond memories of her childhood in
Lockport, plus some insights into her work and the state of
the publishing industry.

US&J: How big a role has Lockport played in your writing?

JCO: Lockport is fairly graphic and clear in some of my writing.
I've also written about places like Detroit, Mich., and I have a novel
set in an area like Princeton. Generally, when the location is not
specified in my writing it takes place in upstate New York. The novel
Marya: A Life is set in that area but I don't name any names. And
You Must Remember This is set in Port Oriskany, an area like Lock-
port and Buffalo, more or less a blend of the two. Rather more
Lockport. Almost as if Lockport had the heavy industry Buffalo had.

US&J: To what degree do your childhood memories get into your
writing?

JCO: I think the memory is always serving us. Sometimes we
think it's imagination when it's really memory. You think you're
inventing something and it turns out you're really remembering
something from your past. Much of it comes out from dreams and
the unconscious.

US&J: When did you decide to become a writer?

JCO: I was always interested in telling stories when I was a child.
And I would draw. It's a general impulse in children. The creative
impulse is in all of us. Children are very spontaneous, they dance and
sing and tell little stories and do drawings. The degree that serious
artists maintain that spontaneity and playfulness really shapes their
career. It just undergoes transformations as they grow up. That
impulse is in all of us and it begins in childhood.

US&J: What kinds of things did you write as a child?

JCO: I don't remember now. I don't suppose they were much
different than what other children write.

US&J: What kinds of things did you like to read?

JCO: I read *Alice in Wonderland*. I still have the copy of it my grandmother gave me. I read many, many things. I would go to the Lockport Public Library and take out books from the children's department all the time.

US&J: Read any good books lately?

JCO: I'm reading all the time. I just read Italo Calvino's *Invisible Cities*. I have a new biography of Jean Stafford I'm reading. Ray and I just read all the time.

US&J: Which of your characters is most like you?

JCO: That's hard. I've created so many characters. Some of the personality of Marya and some of the personality of Enid in *You Must Remember This*, they're both like me. But not entirely. The sensitivity of both Marya and Enid resembles my own. The perceptions they have of the world. When Enid is wandering around Lockport, looking at the canal, going over the footbridge; that's close to me.

US&J: There's not much left of the footbridge.

JCO: I know, it's a shame. We were there about six months ago and I was walking in that area. I was amazed that anything remains from that time. The area hasn't changed that much. There's something about Lockport. I really love it. I love the look of the houses, the streets. There's something haunting about it, and about other towns, oh, like Catskill, N.Y., where Mike Tyson has lived and trained. Towns that more or less came along at the same time in American history, with the woodframe houses, the way the streets are laid out. They seem very American, like Edward Hopper's paintings.

US&J: You say you write slowly, yet you turn out so much. How does a writer work slowly while publishing as much as you have?

JCO: I think I concentrate more. My time is spent on work rather than dissipated on other things. I had a conference with Martin Scorsese yesterday and we went out to dinner. Film people like him concentrate their time enormously. Scorsese was making a film in Morocco. They were there for four months and they worked all day long, six days a week. Then they come back and they stay in this building and work all the time editing the film. They only come out once in a while to see somebody and have dinner or go to a movie. He works late at night, day after day. I'm not that concentrated because I'm teaching, too, but when a person is creative and has a project, they can work hour after hour after hour. Other people are watching television or going out. They're doing what they want to do. But you can see the contrast of a person who concentrates, how much they get done. Scorsese has done so many films for a man only in his 40s. But he can do it because he works so hard. The same thing is true for a writer. John Updike writes all the time. That's how it's done. Concentration.

US&J: What's a typical day like for you?

JCO: When I'm working on a project intently, I usually get started early in the morning, by 8 or so. I don't even have breakfast, just some tea. I work till maybe 1 o'clock, then have lunch and take a little break in the afternoon. I usually get back to work by 4 and write until dinner. Sometimes I even work after dinner but most of the time we just read then.

US&J: Sounds like a full day.

JCO: Yes, but it doesn't seem so when you have a project. For instance, yesterday I mailed back revisions on a novel. When you have a 400-page novel so close to being done, it's a matter of typing over page 59 and typing over page 312. It's so exciting you can stay up till 2 in the morning doing that. What's hard about writing is beginning a new work because you don't know where you're going. That's hard emotionally and psychologically. First drafts are hard for anyone. Many of my friends say they don't write, they rewrite. But I just spend a week doing revisions, and doing that is so pleasurable, I can work hour after hour without getting tired.

US&J: Is there a work pattern you follow when developing and writing a novel?

JCO: They're all different, I think. Sometimes I sit down and I write a plot in longhand, with little sentences, so it looks like it's flowing, like poetry. And there's a sort of narrative there from the start. Other times it starts off more impressionistic.

US&J: I heard you've abandoned your computer and have gone back to the typewriter.

JCO: I guess I just lost interest in it. I don't dislike the word processor. The situation was that the word processor needed very expensive repairs and it was out of the house. I was working pretty happily at the typewriter, so I felt I didn't need it. And I do a lot of work in longhand anyway, sitting on the sofa with a cat at my side.

US&J: Some critics say you write too much. What would you say to them about that?

JCO: Oh, I don't have any interest in knowing what they say. Critics say—things. Some people don't write enough, maybe some people write too much. It doesn't matter what they say.

US&J: What would you say to those who feel there's too much violence in your writing?

JCO: Again, it doesn't matter. As an American novelist in the '70s and '80s, I'm probably writing about my experience as an American. I don't pretend the violence isn't there. There are some writers who would like to live in a Virginia Woolf kind of refinement. But I'm more or less of the school of the writer as witness. Witness to history and society. On the other hand, when you look at my writing, the proportion of domestic and non-violent pages and scenes is much higher than the violent material.

US&J: Is it just prudery when people say there's too much violence in your work?

JCO: It's probably a little sexist because I don't think they would say that about a male writer. People wouldn't make those comments about Faulkner or Mailer or Hemingway. These things have been said about my writing since 1963 and now it's 1988. But I think as time goes by the subjects women are "allowed" to write about will be broader. Women can write about things other than domestic life.

US&J: One of your recent passions has been a traditionally male subject, boxing. How did you get interested in it?

JCO: My father took me to Golden Gloves tournaments as a girl. We didn't go to see other sports, we didn't see any baseball games, so boxing became the focus.

US&J: What do you think of Mike Tyson?

JCO: He's a very interesting boxer. He's still developing. The problem Tyson has is the same one Joe Louis faced. He doesn't have worthy opponents. And until Tyson has a really worthy opponent, like Muhammad Ali had with Joe Frazier, he can't be a great boxer. He can be a very wonderful boxer, his skills are being developed constantly. He changes from fight to fight and becomes more interesting to watch as he develops. But his opponents are not good enough for him. His next fight, against Michael Spinks, will be a more difficult fight. Tyson will have to do a lot of real boxing.

US&J: Another powerful male. What did you think of Mikhail Gorbachev?

JCO: I was very impressed with Gorbachev as a person, in the flesh, and the way he spoke. He has a very dynamic personality. He's utter sincerity and boundless energy. In person, both he and his wife exuded a charm and directness and even a youthfulness that didn't come across so much by way of the media.

US&J: One critic called you the fourth Bronte sister. Do you take such whimsical nicknames as compliments?

JCO: Oh, yes, that's meant to be a compliment. It was said by one of my Princeton colleagues. The Brontes were great geniuses so it was definitely a compliment.

US&J: You went through more of a romantic period in the early '80s with *Bellefleur* and *A Bloodsmoor Romance*. Now it's said you've turned back to realism with *Marya: A Life* and *You Must Remember This*. Is that an accurate assessment?

JCO: Well, those earlier books are not romantic. They're what could be called post-modernist and experimental. I'm going back to that mode, maybe in 1990. I have two more novels in that series. There's one more realistic novel called *American Appetites* that will come out in January 1989 set in a place like Princeton. It's about an accidental murder, I guess you could call it manslaughter, and the consequences of the trial. After that I'm going back to the experimental novels.

US&J: E.P. Dutton published 50,000 hardcover copies of *You Must Remember This*. That's a big printing. Do you think you're bridging the gap between high-brow and mainstream?

JCO: I don't think I could be a popular writer. My writing's too difficult. *Bellefleur* was a best-seller and there were 100,000 copies in print, and when it went into paperback, I think there were a million copies in print. My secret feeling is that people bought the book and couldn't finish it. This happens with some best-sellers that are literary and are long and difficult. I think people go out and buy the book and they try to read it a little but they lose interest. I would guess this happened with Norman Mailer's *Ancient Evenings*. People are well-intentioned, but I don't think there are that many serious readers in the country. We're talking about books that make a serious demand on the reader in terms of time and in terms of thinking. So I don't

think I could ever be a popular writer, except maybe with the suspense novels I've been doing under a pseudonym. I'm publishing
another novel next year as Rosamond Smith. It's a suspense novel,
sort of a terrifying story. It's got a real plot, like a movie, scene one,
scene two, a lot of dialogue. It moves along telling a story the way a
movie would.

US&J: Sounds like the first one you wrote as Rosamond Smith,
Lives of the Twins. The demands on the reader weren't as great.

JCO: That's right, it's much easier reading. *Lives of the Twins* was
also condensed in *Cosmopolitan*, and the editors there know their
audience isn't a group of heavy literary readers.

US&J: Your regular publisher, Dutton, and your agent were
peeved when they learned you had sold a book under a pseudonym,
and to a different publisher.

JCO: Oh, they were horrified. They said lots of things. It was one
of the most unpleasant days of my life. I had thought that if I used a
pseudonym, it would stay secret and no one would ever know. I
really didn't intend anything bad, nothing malicious or evil or wicked.
It just turned out that people interpreted it the wrong way. I didn't
want to make any money. I just wanted a new identity, kind of a
freshness to have a book come out where nobody was comparing it
to other books. "Here's a new novel by blank; just look at the book."
When you get a reputation, like Saul Bellow or Updike, every book
you bring out is referred to your other writing. You can't escape your
identity. That's very frustrating. I wanted to focus on the sheer book
itself—and it's not even any kind of a pretentious book. It's just a little
book, telling a story. But it all backfired on me. It was very unpleasant. Dutton is publishing the next one I'm doing under a
pseudonym, so it's not so bad now.

US&J: What's happening with the movie deals on your novels?

JCO: Well, *Lives of the Twins* has been optioned for a movie. And
Scorsese for *You Must Remember This*. He's going to produce it but
he's just finishing up a project now and then he's got another movie.
So it probably won't be until late 1989, which is fine with me
because if I do the screenplay, I'll need a lot of time.

US&J: Is this a healthy time for American literature?

JCO: I think so. There are many new paperback series that are
offshoots of hardcover publishers. They bring out attractive books.

People are buying them. A lot of my friends are being published in them. They're not exactly mass market paperbacks, they don't have that pulpy look. They're quality paperbacks. Those seem to be really selling well.

US&J: So you think there's plenty of room for quality writing among the supermarket checkout bestsellers.

JCO: Well, you have to remember that Stephen King and other popular writers keep the industry going. The best-selling books, whether they're diet books or horror books or spy novels, they keep bookstores open. I think literary people have to acknowledge that. I'm surrounded by poets, for instance, who don't understand that poetry does not pay its own way. If you're a publisher like Random House or Dutton or Viking, of course you're going to publish Stephen King. With the millions and millions of dollars you've made with him, you can also publish poetry, you can publish the first novel by a young writer. Without this setup, there wouldn't be any industry. I'm not the kind of literary writer who makes sardonic comments about the others. We need them.

US&J: What advice do you give to young writers?

JCO: Just to write. The literal practice of writing, putting words down, getting a first draft. If you get a first draft, then you start feeling a little surge of power. You feel kind of happy about it, so you'll go on to the second draft. It's like if you want to be an athlete, you have to go into training. You can't just think about it. If you want to be a jogger, you just go out one morning and run 10 minutes. Then the next morning you run 20 minutes. You have to build up. Just do it. Write. And do a lot of reading, eclectic reading. Go to the bookstore and buy a lot of paperbacks by people you've never heard of. Have an open and free attitude because writing should be playful and fun.

US&J: For which of your books do you most want to be remembered?

JCO: *You Must Remember This.* It's just closest to me. Lockport, New York, which we all love, is sort of bound up in its pages. I have a lot of personal memories in there. I feel it's a novel that deals with society and politics and various themes that are close to me.

Oates Writes out of "Fascination," not Zeal

George Myers, Jr./1989

From *The Columbus Dispatch*, 5 February 1989, 9F. © 1989 *The Columbus Dispatch*. Reprinted by permission.

Sheer devotion to her art, and energy. It adds up. By now, there is no emotion and few subjects that Joyce Carol Oates hasn't tackled, and she's written about them all marvelously, whether it be boxing, cars, feminist criticism or *Alice in Wonderland*.

And then there's her fiction. Oates, author of 19 novels and many volumes of short stories, essays, plays and poems, most recently published *The Assignation* (Ecco, $16.95) and *American Appetites* (Dutton, $18.95).

American Appetites is about Ian and Glynnis McCullough, happily married until suspicion enters their lives and ruins them. They haven't the imagination to rescue themselves from a banal existence and so into a myriad of terrible eddies they go. In a single spasm of violence, all is lost; one dies.

The Assignation, a gathering of shorter fictions, runs the gamut— violent rummagings of the heart, a father dies, cruising bars. Last year's *(Woman) Writer: Opportunities and Occasions* (Dutton, $18.95) is the latest book to collect Oates' insightful—and highly intuitive—musings on literature and life in subjects varied as the city of Detroit, the novel *Frankenstein* and Kafka.

In the following interview, excerpted from an exchange of letters, Oates talks about what it means to be a reader, writer and critic.

Q. In *(Woman) Writer*, you say: "A woman who writes is a writer by her own definition; but she is a *woman* writer by others' definitions." Why do so many male reviewers refer to what they see as your "prodigious output" in their opening gambits? Perhaps women critics do, too, but I'm not aware of it.

A. Perhaps it is "unfeminine" to seem to be energetic and productive, and male reviewers feel obliged to speak on this issue rather than more female reviewers do. In fact, I work so hard on my

181

books—my activity isn't so much writing as rewriting—that the enterprise is a matter of stubbornness and devotion more than prodigious energy of any sort. Writing is primarily the attempt to re-create an interior vision in an exterior form—that is, in words. How easy to state, yet how hard to accomplish.

Q. Does a man's review of your novels and essays have somehow less veracity than a woman's? And, if a male reader comes away from one of your books with a different view of what he's experienced than a woman, do you think the male has missed something?

A. No, I don't believe a man's interpretation of my writing has less veracity than a woman's. I don't feel at all distant from, and certainly not adversarial to, men: I am close to my father, have been married for 28 years (to the same man), and have many men friends. I value male writers as highly as women writers and have probably made no real distinction between them over the years. Male response to my *On Boxing* was generous and even, in some quarters, extremely enthusiastic. The late Jim Jacobs, co-manager of Mike Tyson, became a friend of mine as a consequence of his admiration for my boxing writing, and Jim was probably the most critical, keen-eyed interpreter of that sport. Probably it is a matter of a reader/reviewer's personal nature: Is he or she inclined to be sympathetic and generous, or is he or she inclined to be grudging, distrustful, at times resentful? Some of my finest critics, in fact, have been men, now that I consider the question.

Q. What should literary criticism be, at its best?

A. At its best, literary criticism should be a means of expanding our knowledge of and appreciation of literature. In America, no one needs to be told not to buy a book—thus combative criticism is fairly pointless.

Q. In an issue of *Ontario Review* (which Oates edits), Elaine Showalter writes: "The first responsibility of the feminist critic with regard to serious women's writing is to buy it; the second, to enlarge the sympathies of the audience." Do you agree, and how is feminist criticism different than criticism?

A. Feminist criticism, at least the kind Showalter speaks of, has tended to be supportive, sympathetic, educational, analytical—and has focussed upon discovering, or rediscovering, women's texts that have been neglected. Anzia Yezierska (1885-1970), Charlotte Perkins

Gilman (1860-1935), Zora Neale Hurston (1901-1960)—and many others—are women who have been "re" discovered by feminists; and other writers, known, but not well-known, have benefited from feminist attention. It was a highly promotional cover story on Alice Walker, in *Ms. Magazine*, that launched *The Color Purple*, for instance.

Q. As a writer, do you experience life as it happens, or not till a residuum of it is transcribed onto the page?

A. Probably both. This is the human predilection: for life as it is 'legended', meditated upon afterward. (The motive for sportswriting and -reading, after all: No one reads the sports pages more avidly than those who have already seen the games.)

Q. How much of your novels are rewritten and reworked?

A. My novels are endlessly rewritten as they are written—page by page. After I have a completed draft, I set the manuscript aside for some weeks; then usually rewrite entirely. Some novels were written over a period of years, in segments—*Marya: A Life*, for instance— then rewritten once I had a seemingly complete draft assembled. I write in longhand first, then at the typewriter. Though I have a reputation (strange and uncanny, to me) for being prolific, in fact I write very slowly; and am likely to spend an entire morning on a single page. I love poetry because it is there, seemingly, to be re-written: over and over, until it strikes the ear as right.

Q. Do you ever let go of a manuscript still wondering about some passage or other in it, mystified by what you've written, or wondering if it works? I wonder especially about the more tissuey narrative structures of some of your earlier books, where you seemed to be writing out of a daydream. Successfully, and yet entranced.

A. No, not really. Like Virginia Woolf, who stated quite explicitly that she wanted to seem effortless, as if writing swiftly, I do a good deal of conscious editing. My earlier books were all much longer, and shortened in the process of rewriting. *Expensive People*, for instance, was another novel entirely: in the rewriting, the most crucial element, the voice, was substantially altered. Now, with more experience, I seem to be capable of "editing" in my head—not putting down so much first-draft material that, in the end, will have to be eliminated.

Q. A quotidian question: With all that you're writing—essays, reviews, novels and screenplays—how do you plan a workday?

A. When I am writing a novel, I keep to a fairly disciplined schedule; out of a fascination for what I am doing rather more than a sense of puritanical zeal. When I am not writing a novel, I am likely to follow my intuition, but mornings are usually reserved for writing of one kind or another—reviews, letters, revisions or poems, draftings of possible stories and novels. (I have many more pages of "plans" in my drawers than I will ever live to execute, I'm afraid. Some of the plans are quite systematical and elaborate.)

Q. I read you are writing the screenplay for *You Must Remember This*. Are you doing so to keep the book "yours," or is it that you want to try something new, or need a break from fiction? I understand there's a certain comfort in working with characters you already know so well.

A. I am working with Martin Scorsese on the screenplay, and the experience has been extremely interesting. Of course, movies are not novels; they must be autonomous creations, and no novel's texture of language can be conveyed to the screen. I love transposing stories I know very well into visual terms, but I am not certain that I would want to write an "original" screenplay.

Q. Were you displeased with the screen treatment of your short story, "Where Are You Going, Where Have You Been?"

A. Joyce Chopra and Tom Cole did a remarkable job of transposing an essentially untranslatable short story into film. "Where Are You Going, Where Have You Been?" was conceived of as an allegory of sorts—a contemporary version of *Death and the Maiden*; legends (though I was thinking of woodcuts); and *Smooth Talk*, while retaining some of that eerie other-worldliness, is fundamentally a realistic film, filled with marvelous little details. Far from being displeased, I was quite impressed with the film. And, as I've said, a movie is an autonomous creation—not an aspect of prose. I could have wished, perhaps, for a different ending to the film, but I suppose that the ending I wrote was simply not translatable; or palatable.

Q. Has there ever been a good book, a good work of art, that you read and wished terribly to alter or change in some way: *Nostromo? Moby-Dick? Alice in Wonderland?*

A. I am not by nature a contentious person; I tend to grant the writer his or her vision, perhaps because, as a writer, I know how terribly difficult it can be, sometimes, to simply write. I've written on all three of the books you mention, and admire them enormously.

Q. Does the experience of reading satisfy you, or make you restless, perhaps to in some way continue the text through criticism or review of it?

A. This is a good issue: I tend to think that exciting reading stimulated writing; not imitation so much as a sense of transcendent pleasure in the possibility of making something permanent, or semipermanent, out of the ephemera of our lives. Though there are writers deathly in their influence—Dylan Thomas, Emily Dickinson, perhaps Faulkner—because they are so extraordinarily good—we can yet be moved by them to write out of our own very different visions.

Q. To an adult who has not known the pleasures of reading—someone who suddenly wished to read—what texts would you recommend, and why these?

A. I don't believe I understand the question. "Serious" writing, do you mean? One should always begin with contemporary work, since all writers write for their contemporaries. (That is, Charles Dickens is now a "classic"—but was not so in his own lifetime. He wrote for his own time, not for posterity.) Thus it is not a generally sound idea for people unfamiliar with serious writing to begin with the old, revered "classic"—they might work their way back to them, perhaps. Though *Huckleberry Finn* is a classic that has the immediacy and power of a contemporary work, and might well be the starting-off place for a reader of the sort you hypothesize.

Index